AROUND THE U.S.A.

IN 1,000 PICTURES

AROUND THE U.S.A.
IN 1,000 PICTURES

A PHOTOGRAPHIC ENCYCLOPEDIA
OF TRAVEL IN THE UNITED STATES

Edited by A. MILTON RUNYON
and VILMA F. BERGANE

FOREWORD BY PAUL J. C. FRIEDLANDER
10 MAPS DRAWN BY RAFAEL PALACIOS

NELSON DOUBLEDAY, INC.
Garden City, N.Y.

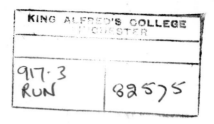
FOR DAVID AND JAMES

ACKNOWLEDGMENTS

The editors wish to thank *The New York Times* and
the authors for permission to reprint the following
articles, copyright 1954 by *The New York Times:*
New England, by John H. Fenton; *The Midsouth,* by
Stacy V. Jones; *The South,* by John Popham; *The
Midwest,* by Richard J. H. Johnston; *The Plains
States,* by Seth S. King; *The Rocky Mountains,* by
Marshall Sprague; *The Southwest,* and *Southern Cali-
fornia,* by Gladwin Hill; *California—The Golden
Gate,* by Lawrence E. Davies; *The Northwest,* by
Richard L. Neuberger. All other rights in these articles
are specifically reserved to the authors.

Library of Congress Catalog Card Number 56–8486
PRINTED IN THE UNITED STATES

Title page photo: Mount Shuksan, Washington, by Walt Dyke

At cherry blossom time, Jefferson Memorial area is Washington's top attraction.

CONTENTS

Photo: Lincoln Statue, Lincoln Memorial, by Capt. M. W. Arps, U.S.N. Ret.

"FROM SEA TO SHINING SEA" —THE MOODS OF AMERICA

by Paul J. C. Friedlander

For the purposes of the tourist, "America the Beautiful," as described in the Katharine Lee Bates poem and song from which the heading of this Foreword is taken, consists of eleven separate regions. Each is as big as, if not bigger than, many world powers. Each is an entity in itself. Each has a personality, and characteristics of geography and agriculture, of people and industry, of scenery and climate—both physical and intellectual—that make it distinct from all other regions. Just as the traveler can tell when he crosses from England to Wales or from German Switzerland into Italian Switzerland, so he can tell in this country without recourse to an atlas when he is in New England, the Midsouth or the Deep South.

To aid the vacationist about to plan a tour of his own country, the armchair traveler anxious to learn more about his native land, and the returned traveler who wants to kindle anew the memories of the places he has visited, the editors of this book have selected well over a thou-

Mr. Friedlander is Travel Editor, The New York Times

sand pictures showing America in its many moods, at work and at play. They have identified each picture with pertinent and often intriguing facts. And they have reprinted with permission character studies of the eleven regions written by correspondents of *The New York Times* who live and work in the various sections they describe.

Because the editors have already covered in their previous book, *Around the World in 1,000 Pictures,* such outlying sections of the United States as Alaska, Hawaii, Puerto Rico and the Virgin Islands, this book deals principally with the 48 states and the District of Columbia. Emphasis is placed on the natural wonders of our country and the places of greatest interest to the pleasure traveler and the vacationist. Yet these alone cannot convey the moods of America. The strength and spirit of our country today are

Cape Perpetua, Oregon, was discovered by Captain Cook, named for St. Perpetua.

compounded of 160,000,000 people and of their forebears, and of the things they believed in and worked and fought for, the same principles we honor today at our historic shrines.

So among these 1,000 photographs you will find more than the grandeur of nature as it spreads in a 3,000-mile panorama from sea to shining sea. You will see many of the great historic shrines that bring to life those great occasions in New England, Pennsylvania, Virginia and in many other regions when Americans wrote the history of the New World in bold, unfrightened hands. You'll see their descendants at work today—on the farms, in the automobile factories and the industries that make this nation, and the fishermen who still go down to the sea under sail. And, to complete the picture, you'll see Americans at play

in their National Parks where the wilderness of this continent is preserved as it was when the first explorers and hunters came through; on the broad sandy beaches that encircle this land like a golden necklace; and at the fabulous man-made resorts like Reno and Palm Springs and Miami Beach, and the biggest tourist attraction of them all—New York City.

Many of the pictures were taken by world-famous photographers, but most of them were made by men and women who live in the various regions and have had the opportunity to capture on film the places they love best. The photos have been selected, not for the qualities that would win prizes in a competition, but for their ability to show America's colorful scenes and people and events in the same way you might like to preserve them in your own photo album. This is a tremendous undertaking, to picture this great nation in one volume. To do it as successfully as they have, the editors had to touch lightly, or not at all, a few sections of the country. They beg, herewith, the indulgence of the loyal partisans thereof.

It is their hope, and I commend this volume to you in the belief that they have achieved their goal, that this book will help Americans to become more familiar with their own ball park, our friends abroad to see us in our true lights, and inspire both to travel from sea to shining sea to see for themselves the great sights pictured in these pages.

Photo: C. F. Palmer

Pemaquid Point, Maine, extends far out from the bordering land, with a heavy surf pounding continuously on its gray-green rocks. On page 11 is shown the lighthouse that warns ships away. A vast expanse of "shining sea" sweeps into the distance.

East Corinth, Vermont, is typical of the tiny villages that dot the New England landscape, with white colonial houses clustered around a white steepled church.

NEW ENGLAND

by JOHN H. FENTON

The westward migration across America opened new lands and new vistas for a growing population. Among the pioneers who opened the new country were Yankees. But sooner or later the Yankees' descendants come back to New England, if only for a visit. And along with them come other Americans, for this relic-filled corner of the United States exerts a compelling influence. So much of it, from the Atlantic's breakers and Old North Church to the piny hills and bouldered fields and the Yankees themselves, has been changeless for 300 years.

The sounds of New England are many: the wind in the sand dunes of Cape Cod, the water lapping the sun-bleached fishing wharves of Maine, the rush of a mountain-fed stream in New Hampshire and the twitter of birds in the Berkshire hills of Massachusetts. Voices from the past whisper in the Colonial burying grounds of Boston, in the House of Seven Gables in Salem, beneath the bridge at Concord and in the Old Stone Mill at Newport.

The architecture is a conglomerate blend of graceful Colonial, sterner Federal, utilitarian Cape Cod and the best and worst of the contemporary. In places like Boston, Newburyport and Newport it is possible to turn a corner and go back 300 years.

By and large, the native Yankee has been pictured as a bleak character, with an inborn suspicion of all strangers, inhospitable and clannish. Actually, by nature and heritage, he has a respect for individual opinion. And he is inclined to keep the latchstring of his hospitality withdrawn on the theory that he himself would not knock without good reason.

There are many aspects to this region,

Vermont farm in winter: Central part of the state averages ten feet of snow cover.

but a specific tradition marks New England as the national cornerstone. It is found in Boston, in Lexington, in Concord, in Bennington and Newport and Salem. Visitors from all over the world have come to see the shrines and view the relics of the American Revolution that changed the trend of history.

They walk the Boston streets where British muskets rattled in the massacre. They climb the stairs of the Old North Church where the signal lights for Paul Revere were hung. They drive through the Middlesex countryside where the hoofs of Revere's horse echoes in the night. They visit Plymouth and walk where the Pilgrims marched to church. And they wander through a hundred churchyards where fading slate stones tell the story of departed pioneers and patriots.

The United Nations Building dominates the East River waterfront of midtown New York, seen from the opposite shore. Empire State Building towers at far left.

Some of New York's most spectacular views are from the top of the RCA Building in Rockefeller Center. Empire State mast glows red at night to warn airplanes.

Photos: Shostal; H. S. Crocker

MID-ATLANTIC STATES

by PAUL J. C. FRIEDLANDER

The Middle Atlantic States—New York, New Jersey, Pennsylvania and Delaware —constitute a kind of old, established and, therefore, respectable *avant garde* of the United States of America. They set the pace for the rest of the country in finance, communications, industry, science, education, and in the civilizing influences of culture and of fashions.

With their roots deep in the history of pre-Colonial days, these four states need not bluster over their origins, their patriotism or devotion to America's ideals, for they were among the very first to fight for, achieve and practice them since the days when this continent was parceled out in royal grants. They are able to face life more calmly, with the stability of a mature population, than some of their sovereign cousins to the west. Their outlook is of necessity broader, international and global because of their vantage point on the Atlantic seaboard.

The highest compliment a visitor can give a San Franciscan is to tell him that his city has the feel, the pace of an eastern metropolis. A traveler through the United States, and particularly an Easterner come home again, immediately feels this drive, this concentration of purposeful energy that moves people, that gets things done. This is the keen spirit of the "major league" of accomplishment, the sophistication of a cruelly competitive market for talent and ideas.

Here, too, are the universities, the book publishing houses, the newspaper and magazine offices where much of the nation's thinking is shaped. Here are headquarters for the media of communications—radio, television, advertising, entertainment. Here are the highest buildings, the deepest subways; the largest cities and biggest seaside playgrounds,

and even deserted, barren areas remote in time and customs, if not miles, from seaboard civilization. Here are the largest banks, the biggest corporations, the richest of the rich, and just down the block in cold-water hovels the poorest of the poor. Here parade the intellectuals and the very smartest smart set and, by extension of this law of superlatives, the dumbest of the dumbbells.

The region owes much of its character to the Appalachian Mountain Range that runs from northeast to southwest, paralleling the Atlantic Coast. They were a barrier against the earliest arrivals, forced the colonizers to build cities and towns on the coastal plain. The few water gaps to the west channeled trade and commerce to and from the great deep-water ports of New York, Newark and Philadelphia, making these big cities grow bigger than ever.

Over 30 million people—one-fifth of the nation's total population—live in these four states, a population cosmopolitan because of the diversity of its origins, yet homogeneous in the sense of being "Easterners." Immigrants and sons of immigrants sit in the legislatures, on the courts and in the governors' mansions, and so do descendants of the men who signed the Declaration of Independence. There are regional and city accents within each state; election campaigns show conflicts between farmers and industrial centers.

Perhaps it is these great diversities in such a great concentration of people in a comparatively small area that gives this region its peculiar character—not as a cross section of America, not the common denominator, but rather a kind of show window of what this country has been, what it is and what it can hope to be.

Costumes of the period, and an old coach, give an early eighteenth-century air to this view of the Governor's Palace at Williamsburg, Virginia. The Palace was reconstructed in 1930 to look as much as possible as it did when finished in 1720.

THE MIDSOUTH

by STACY V. JONES

The Midsouth is New England with the corners rounded. It is more Colonial than Confederate, and this in spite of the fact that roadside markers recall Manassas and Appomattox. Perhaps it would be fairer to call New England a rough-edged Midsouth, for the adventurous businessmen of Jamestown did beat the Puritans to the New World by a few years. At any rate, there are similarities between the two regions: oldness and reverence for age; a pervading sense of duty and the fitness of things; close identification with the finding and founding of America and with the Revolutionary War.

The tourist is likely to see more boxwood than battlefields, for much of the area's history is preserved in the old homes and gardens of the men who made it. Energetic clubwomen have restored numerous eighteenth-century mansions; they collect visitors' half-dollars and see that everything indoors is dusted and everything outdoors is green. Stratford Hall, on Virginia's northern neck, was the birthplace of Robert E. Lee, and also of two earlier Lees, who signed the Declaration of Independence. There is George Washington's birthplace on what was once Pope's Creek and his later home at Mount Vernon on the Potomac; George Mason's Gunston Hall just below the latter, and Jefferson's Monticello at Charlottesville. A whole Colonial capital has been restored at Williamsburg. And colonial plantation houses dot Maryland's Eastern Shore and the banks of the James in Virginia.

Mount Vernon was George Washington's later home and place of burial. It is on Potomac, 14 miles south of Washington.

The Midsouth has great topographic variety, which makes it congenial country for casual touring. In orderly progression tidewater plains cut by widening estuaries give way to rising piedmont farmland, which in turn is broken by the wooded Appalachians—a handsome but tamed range in these parts, well suited to vacationing. And of course there is Washington, a national capital but definitely a Southern city.

Brulatour Courtyard is one of the lovely patios of the *Vieux Carré* in New Orleans, at 520 Royal Street. It is perhaps the city's most painted and photographed patio.

THE SOUTH

by JOHN POPHAM

The South is a kaleidoscopic parade of natural scenery and human attitudes, both of them etched sharply. The land and the people are undergoing great economic and social changes. The past and the present tilt lances in a setting as colorful as any pageantry in history.

The South is a land rich with historical continuity, a land of long days, bright in the sun and slow to cool in the evening shadows. On a summer's day the heat dances visibly along macadamized highways and dusty country roads. The ubiquitous screen doors shut with loud report on hollow stillness. Soft Southern voices add to the muted effect.

Everywhere there is a sense of something old and stable. Go west in North Carolina through the Great Smokies to Cherokee at twilight and watch Cherokee Indians from the near-by reservation act out the tragic story of their ancestors' trek across the "trail of tears" in the days of Andrew Jackson.

Then go down into the valley where the Tennessee River forms the famous Moccasin Bend at Chattanooga and visit the great dams of the Tennessee Valley Authority, where turbines and generators pour out the electrical power that has helped remake the face of this section.

At Memphis one reaches the banks of the Mississippi River and for miles around the country is flat, the soil black with Old Man River's largesse. This bustling city is a modern commercial hub for much of Tennessee, Mississippi and Arkansas but over its business section there yet remains the aura of plantation society. Along the river front cotton is yet the economic king. The shouts of river roustabouts have long since drifted downwind, side-wheelers no longer churn muddy waters and W. C. Handy's jazz is held in escrow on LP records. But trucks loaded with Negro handlaborers still roll out of the city for chopping and weeding in the cotton fields. Men with necks burned red from the sun, wearing broad-brimmed hats and white shirts with open collars, shop in the stores and talk incessantly of cotton prices and Government parity programs.

Southward from Memphis the hand of history remains heavy, but it is the clash of old and new architecture that catches the eye. There are the great pillared mansions in Vicksburg and Natchez, vast stretches of delta cotton land, dotted with sharecroppers' cabins.

New Orleans is a special South within the South. The gems of architecture of the French quarter are perhaps unmatched in this country. Eighty miles upriver is Baton Rouge, where Huey Long built a skyscraper capitol.

The Gulf Coast makes a wide arc from Biloxi to the southern tip of Florida's west coast, a coastal vacation land running down to the citrus groves and cattle farms and thriving tourist towns of Florida.

For all the changes, when the midday sun has softened, when afternoon shadows dapple tree-shaded streets; when children return to play after their naps, there is always a Savannah or Charleston with red-brick sidewalks and colonial architecture and patio gardens to take the visitor back into the past of the South.

Looking east along the Chicago River and Wacker Drive, you see why Chicago is known as a city of bridges. The river is important channel for barge, ship traffic.

The 209-foot-high tower of Rockefeller Memorial Chapel dominates the Midway of the University of Chicago. Chapel has 64-bell carillon, beautiful stained glass.

Photos: Wm. H. Nawodylo, Egon Berka

THE MIDWEST

by RICHARD J. H. JOHNSTON

Midwest farms feed nearly 29 million cattle, almost a third of the nation's total.

Contrary to popular misconception, the Midwest, from the lakes of Minnesota and Wisconsin and the Great Lakes down through Illinois and Indiana and Ohio, is not barren flat land, always more of the same. There is, perhaps, more homogeneity in the people who live in these states than in their landscapes, though the contrasts between the big cities and the rural areas is as sharp as that between one section of this country and another.

For variety, there are in Indiana and Michigan those strange natural wonders, the sand dunes along the eastern shore of Lake Michigan.

One would normally expect the tang of salt air and the roar of ocean surf beyond the dunes, but instead the lake lies quietly in midsummer, shimmering in the sun. Like an isolated world by itself stands the dune country; similarly the Midwest stands almost as distinctly a sheltered world of its own within the United States.

The approach from the East leads through industrial Ohio, then rural Indiana, and then the traveler plunges into the seemingly endless expanse of smoking mills that border Lake Michigan near the Illinois line. Here the great works of the country's major steel companies belch soot and flames, fouling the air and the approach that catapults the motorist suddenly from a maze of factories onto Chicago's South Lake Shore Drive.

In Wisconsin, northern Michigan and Minnesota, the country turns woodsy and green, sprinkled with lakes and fishing streams and with wilderness as unspoiled as it was when the French missionaries and explorers and fur traders first opened up this territory. South in Illinois, across the prairie, one reaches the Abraham Lincoln country and the shrines at Springfield.

The Mississippi by now has run its majestic course down through the bluffs and is flowing smoothly across the flat country beyond which the prairie runs off through Iowa into the neighboring Plains States. The nation's railroads and airlines spoke out from the Midwest, her products and her cities feed the nation's industry and commerce.

This is a cross-section of latter-day America. Once the wild Northwest Territory, it has long been tamed. It lacks the majesty of some other regions; it is America at home and at work. After all, the internal combustion engine and the automobile, the truck and powered farm implements and the mail order house—developments that made possible the present state of America at home and abroad—came out of the Midwest.

North Dakota Ranch: The state's cattle raising, with nearly two million head, is centered in Missouri Valley. Finest farm land is in celebrated Red River Valley.

Chateau de Mores, with its 28 rooms, was built near Medora, North Dakota, by the spirited young Marquis de Mores when he built a packing plant in the cattle country.

THE PLAINS STATES

by SETH S. KING

The moment a traveler crosses the Mississippi River and heads west he begins to encounter the one dominant quality of the Plains States—space. Starting with the rolling, compact corn fields and pasture lands of Iowa, and extending beyond the Missouri River to the great wheat plains and ranges of Nebraska, Kansas, and the Dakotas, his horizon broadens until it is almost limitless.

From the rich black and green of the corn country he moves into the grayer, lighter green and gold of the wheat lands and then to the brown ranges that stretch clear to the foot of the dark blue mountains. From the great white barns and silos of Iowa and Minnesota, past the towering grain elevators and sprawling feed lots of eastern Nebraska and Kansas, the traveler crosses on to the Great Plains, where the small ranch houses and corrals are almost lost in the expanse of land.

In the Plains States, people earn their living from the land; they do not merely live on it. Because of this, the people change as the land changes.

In Iowa there is a tendency toward conservatism. Here the people have been established for several generations, and they are more secure in the knowledge that theirs is one of the most consistently productive farm areas in the world. Beyond the Missouri, nature is more uncertain. As the yearly rainfall diminishes, the gamble on livelihood or even on survival increases. The people more often are imbued with a casual disregard for formality and are generally sustained by a persistent optimism. Still farther to the west, the land becomes rougher. It makes a greater demand on the people there, and they, like their pioneer fathers, take pride in having withstood the fierce winter

Combine cuts a wide swath through golden wheat of an enormous Plains States farm.

blizzards, the dust and the summer heat. They are marked by their independence.

The great sweep of plains from the Missouri westward to the Rockies is a relatively new country. But it is rich with the history of this nation's drive toward the Pacific. And most of its sections are still wild enough for a traveler to visualize, with ease, the wagon trains that once labored over the plains or the keel boats and war canoes that struggled up the rivers in search of a route to the Western Sea.

The great expanses of North and South Dakota beyond the Missouri can also be fascinating, if one looks across the unbroken rangeland and remembers that the wild Sioux Indians once came plunging over these same rolling hills in pursuit of buffalo or the white man.

Chair lift gives a spectacular view of Jackson, Wyoming, and the Grand Tetons. One of the West's most interesting frontier towns, Jackson is a sports paradise.

The Grand Canyon of the Yellowstone changes color constantly, with lighting and perspective, running through shades of yellow, orange, red, purple and brown.

Photos: H. S. Crocker; Josef Muench

THE ROCKY MOUNTAINS

by MARSHALL SPRAGUE

I regained my health a dozen years ago in the Rockies and perhaps that is why I can't imagine enjoying life unless I'm a mile or so up in the air with my pulse clipping along at 90 or 100 to the minute. I am nuts about the Rockies and about the altitude which gives a special quality to this whole vast beautiful region from Colorado to the Sierras, from New Mexico to Montana.

Life is simpler, for one thing. The mountains are majestic, simple forms, easy on the eye and mind. It rarely rains so we have no dank vegetation to worry about or many bugs or varieties of birds. We don't have to garden or go swimming or build gutters around our houses if we don't want to. The river systems are so few that my own town of Colorado Springs names its principal streets after them and my children can name every river and most of the creeks between here and Spokane. Though our cities are growing to beat the band, they are not crowded in the eastern sense and we don't ever think they will be unless someone invents a machine to manufacture water.

The scarcity of people makes mountain society more relaxed than sea-level society or middle west society. I don't think Rocky Mountain dwellers are kinder or more generous or more hospitable or more honest than New Yorkers. But they are easier to know on brief acquaintance, less suspicious of motives, less reserved, less jumpy. I am told that bear and buffalo never fled from the first hunters out here because it did not occur to them that anyone would want to harm them. Mountaineers are a bit like that today. I notice often how Broadway plays depicting big-city tension—like "Season in the Sun" or "Light Up the Sky" bewilder audiences in Denver or Colorado Springs. Such tension is unfamiliar to them.

We tend to take things easy. Nobody runs for a bus because if he does, he'll have to spend the rest of the day catching his breath. Sports are on the reflective side. We fish for trout in the clear, blue, cold, rippling rivers, some of which we can jump across. We ride horses in the vast clean parks, liking the smell of horses and sage and the look of the sky bluing deeply at the edges. We explore old mining roads in jeeps and we climb mountains which sounds hard but isn't —not the slow way we do it. We picnic a lot. Many towns out this way own pleasant picnic grounds in the hills.

I'll tell you frankly, though, I'd stay East for eating. In season our lettuce, celery, cantaloupe and peas are superb, but beef is seldom first rate because this is where cattle are grown, not fattened. Chickens and pork are so-so, fresh eggs a gamble. Naturally under these conditions good chefs are rare. They just won't stay around and be unhappy working with inferior materials.

People seem to get fresh ideas in the mountains. Every summer a remarkable industrialist named Walter Paepke finances a kind of think center called The Institute for Humanistic Studies in the mining town of Aspen, Colorado, beneath the Elk Mountains. Other industrialists come out for weeks to sit around and talk to each other and to professional thinkers and to hear good music in a big orange tent. They claim the process lets them see their particular industry in relation to what it can do for all humanity. When they return home, everyone in their industry is apt to be better off because of what Aspen did to them.

THE SOUTHWEST

by GLADWIN HILL

motorist driving across the plateau of
northern Arizona recently halted to secure a rattling trunk-latch. As he turned
to climb back in the car, he was stopped
in his tracks by a strange feeling. It took
him several seconds to realize that he was
experiencing, for the first time in months
and perhaps years, absolute, uninterrupted
silence.

Not only were there no people jabber-
ing, automobiles honking, radios blaring,
sirens screeching, trains roaring, or airplanes droning. There was not, with the
low-lying vegetation, even the sounding
harp for random breezes that punctuate
the remotest forests of the world. There
was only silence.

Yet it was an eloquent silence. It went
a long way toward explaining the impas-
siveness, the contentment even in priva-
tion, of the Navajo, systematically living
a mile or more from his neighbor on that
plateau. It explained generations of cowboys, with their cheerfully lonesome bal-
lads. It explained why a half million
people have vied with the rigors of nature
to achieve the peace of the Arizona desert;
why thousands of others choose to dwell
on the isolated farms and ranches of
New Mexico and west Texas.

"The great open spaces" are what the
Southwest is celebrated for. But it's the
quiet and serenity that give the distances
meaning for humankind.

The wail of a midnight juke box at a
crossroads filling station in New Mexico,
the hearty greeting of a prospector or
rancher as he clumps into the solitary
eat-joint of a sagebrush town, seem to
reverberate more through the cosmos
than the clangor of millions in the
world's cities.

Time moves at a different pace.

Through the clear night air of the desert, the stars speak silently of their in-
comprehensible antiquity. Down the mile-
deep gorge of Grand Canyon lie, layer
upon layer, the ashes of a billion years.
The seasons roll, some wet, some dry.
In the highlands, the winter snows swirl
in. On the plains, the tumbleweeds race
erratically before the winds. Year in and
year out, the sun bakes down, on scat-
tered cottonwoods and live-oaks, on pueblos, shacks, hamlets and towns.

Here the apposition between nature
and men, and between men and other
men, is plainest. The Indians, with their
varied visages and customs, bespeak the
mingling of migrations yet untraced,
from as far away as Asia. In little towns
along the Rio Grande are relics of the
Spanish explorers who trod these self-
same routes long before the Pilgrims
landed. For every modern, busy city like
Phoenix, Albuquerque, and Amarillo,
dozens of places like Tombstone and
Cimarron provide living links with the
cattle-trail and mining-boom days of the
19th century.

The visitor here is not taken for
granted as he would be in Cincinnati or
Dallas. He gets the same incisive once-
over that met passengers alighting from
the stagecoaches. Is he a city slicker,
a card-sharp, a gold-brick salesman—or
someone adaptable to the Southwest community? The wise guy is quickly cut down
to size; the condescending remark boom-
erangs.

The spirit of the region—its great open
spaces, its solitude, its individuality—is
poignantly reflected in one of its com-
monest mannerisms: greetings are effu-
sive, farewells laconic—in the tacit wish
that the absence will be short.

Photo: The Alamo, San Antonio,
by William J. Davis (Shostal)

Half Dome from Sentinel Bridge: This monolith, 4,892 feet high, is probably the grandest rock form in the world. It domi- nates the junction of the Merced River and Tenaya Creek. From the top, climb- ers can see the entire Yosemite Valley

CALIFORNIA—THE GOLDEN GATE

by LAWRENCE E. DAVIES

San Francisco's huge Chinatown has the largest Chinese settlement outside the Orient.

A visitor stood in a crowd of 10,000 in the "Wall Street of the West" not long ago watching a ceremony. The financial district of San Francisco had been driven to distraction for four months by the steady, nerve-fraying pounding of a pile driver while it sank supports for a new skyscraper. Now the job was done, the huge hammer silenced, and San Francisco, true to form, brought out pallbearers, wreaths and eulogists and even put the symbolic remains of Alfred the pile driver on a trans-Pacific liner for burial at sea. The visitor thought he had captured the spirit of this metropolis built on a dozen hills. This spirit is an elusive thing, but fun-loving tolerance surely is an ingredient.

The town shows a maturity greater than that of many older ones. It has stability, based on the knowledge that neither earthquake nor seven disastrous fires could down its spirit. Withal, it has never been afraid to be exuberant.

Fog may account for some of San Francisco's character. The relentless billowing of the fog inward through the mile-wide Golden Gate, sometimes leaving the tips of the Golden Gate Bridge towers hanging like ghostly spires, is a fascinating sight almost every afternoon from mid-June through August.

Lake Tahoe, nestling 7,000 feet high in the Sierras, vineyards and wine cellars, natural wonders like Yosemite, all contribute to the character and spirit of the region. But nothing, in the opinion of this adopted Far Westerner, is more awe-inspiring, more majestic, more likely to instill a sense of humility, than a cathedral-like grove of giant redwoods, "nature's oldest living things."

Beautiful Santa Barbara is the best pre-served, and architecturally one of the fin-est of California's great missions. It is constructed of native sandstone, painte[d] ivory, with red-domed towers, a blendin[g] of old Spanish and Moorish architectur[e].

Photo: Josef Muenc[h]

SOUTHERN CALIFORNIA

by GLADWIN HILL

here is an exotic Oriental dish with some name like mooey-mooey composed f so many ingredients it is said that no wo people have ever agreed on what it asted like.

The same quality is shared, for similar easons, by Southern California. The "S" n Southern California, incidentally, is lways capitalized—in Southern California. It is climatically and culturally quite lifferent from northern California (spelled with a small "n"), which bears it approximately the same relationship as Albany loes to New York City: the legislature meets there.

At first blush, Southern California is a bewildering melange: a land of forested mountains, barren deserts, shimmering seashore . . . of Indians and atomic scientists . . . and the Mexican "wetbacks." People from every state in the union, who annually hold Iowa picnics and New England picnics . . . but who concur that they never had it so good.

Southern California is a melting pot which has not yet come to heat. The population is stratified not economically or socially, but chronologically. There are the Spanish-named Old Families. There are the descendants of the 19th-century pioneers. There are the folks from the big influx of the 1920's, living in an increasingly imaginary world of orange-groves and annuities in 100-cent dollars. There are the Okies of the 1930's—many now prospering entrepreneurs. There are the industrial immigrants of World War II, who hurtled from Alabama's cotton patches to suede shoes in half a decade. And there are the "vets"—the nation's biggest concentration of them—who formed the nucleus of the continuing post-war migration.

The keynote, the strand running through all these diverse elements, is "living." "California living" has become a tag associated with everything from clothes to condiments. It derives primarily from *Southern* California and its bland climate, which encourages people in a thousand pastimes, from skiing to skin-diving, from sun-bathing to salad-making.

The swimming pool is Southern California's trade-mark, not as a badge of affluence (they cost less than a car), but as a symbol of people's defiant devotion, in the frenetic atomic era, to something more than the humdrum business of Making Ends Meet. An even more universal symbol, no longer exclusive to the region but indigenous to it, is the patio. You may stage barbecues in it, or just sit in it, or just have it. The point is that you're proclaiming that there's more to life than four walls and a roof.

"California living" takes many forms, some of them ridiculous. It connotes Pasadena's palm-shaded New England-style houses, their roofs determinedly peaked (by transplanted New Englanders) to shed completely non-existent snows.

It connotes the paradox of the Cadillac, the badge of "arrival" on the one hand in the Hollywood movie colony, and on the other along Central Avenue, Los Angeles' Harlem . . . and in many cases the pickup truck of the large-scale cotton grower, who counts his holdings in square miles.

It isn't the people who are crazy. It's the pattern. The common trait of Southern Californians is that they're all converts. "You may not like it at first," they advise visitors. "But after you've been here awhile—" Once the visitor finds some kind of niche in the pattern, he's set. And pretty soon, he's saying: "You may not like it at first, but—"

Beautiful Spirit Lake, Washington, lies at the foot of Mount St. Helens, volcanic peak that last erupted in 1840. The lake, as deep as 1,300 feet in many places and with some "bottomless" spots, abounds in rainbow and other varieties of trout.

THE NORTHWEST

by RICHARD L. NEUBERGER

Abundance is the dominant impression one gets of the Northwest. Everything is in profusion—trees, wildlife, water, flowered orchards, leaping salmon in the rivers. Even the vast interior desert of sagebrush is split by the mighty Columbia, champing in a deep lava gorge. Irrigation canals have wrested alfalfa fields and symmetrical panels of row crops from the choking grip of cactus and tumbleweed. At no other place in the land does so much annual rainfall descend from the skies as along the Northwest's timbered seacoast. This has produced majestic "rain forests" where Douglas fir giants scrape the heavens.

Seattle, Portland and Spokane are teeming cities, but essentially the realm seems untrammeled. On the Lolo Trail, sheer above Idaho's crystalline Lochsa River, stand rock cairns that helped to guide Lewis and Clark to Oregon, unchanged since the great explorers saw them 150 years ago. The Northwest is that much linked to its frontier beginnings. I have walked along the Lolo, knowing that my shoes were fitting into the bygone moccasin prints of the first of all westbound Americans.

Northwesterners are conscious of the region's hurtling rivers, which claw at granite cliffs with white-capped talons. In this one sprawling region lurks 42 per cent of all the undeveloped hydroelectric power in the United States. The Northwest has no other industrial fuel—no coal, no petroleum, no natural gas. If manufacturing payrolls are to ease the economic pressure on the forests of Oregon and Washington, this will come about only because of the generation of more low-cost water power. Already the rivers that tumble over concrete spillways are

Mt. Rainier looms over Puyallup Valley.

responsible for the major factories that dot the region.

The traveler, looking from his bus seat or Pullman berth, knows clearly when he has come to the Northwest. The trees are thicker, taller and more numerous. The peaks may not be intrinsically as high as those in the Rockies, but their cushion of snow is deeper, their glaciers more active. James Bryce said that nowhere else on the planet were sea and forest and upland so united in a single vernal panorama, and this is the Northwest's ultimate glory.

The Northwest's favorite legend is that of Paul Bunyan, the mighty lumberjack, who used a fir tree for a toothpick and measured the stuffing for his Christmas goose in metric tons. This tells a good deal about the region and its people. Northwesterners were radiant when Hell's Canyon on the Snake River turned out to be a few feet deeper than Grand Canyon on the Colorado River.

Photo: Josef Scaylea

Oregon's Willamette River runs through a valley considered by many travelers to be one of the West's most beautiful Willamette Valley is 180 miles long

Columbia River cuts through majestic Cascade Mountains, with Washington on one side, Oregon on the other. Columbia River highway parallels the great river.

Photos: Ray Atkeson

AROUND THE U.S.A.
IN 1,000 PICTURES

WHAT'S NEW IN THE U.S.A.

New expressways, bridges, and toll roads are making it easier than ever for the people of the U.S. to explore their land. This is new expressway at Kansas City.

Photo: Massie—Missouri Resources Div.

3

Two recent rockfalls at Niagara Falls have altered the appearance of the great American Falls considerably. In July, 1954, an estimated 185,000 tons of rock,

New Marine Corps War Memorial, Va., is based on Rosenthal's Iwo Jima photo.

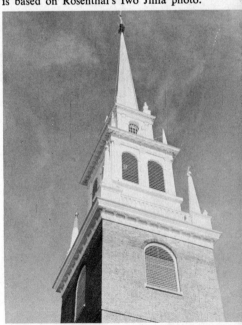

dirt and rubble plunged into the 170-foot deep chasm of the Niagara River gorge.

New steeple on Old North Church, Boston, replaces one hit by 1954 hurricane.

Photos: Grant M. Haist

What's New in the U.S.A.

Walt Disney's Magic Kingdom of Disneyland, at Anaheim, California, is newest amusement park for young and old. This is the "Turn of the Century" Main Street.

A "real" pirates' galleon sits at anchor in Disneyland courtyard, sails a-billow.

Lifelike alligators "threaten" the sightseeing boat on the river at Disneyland.

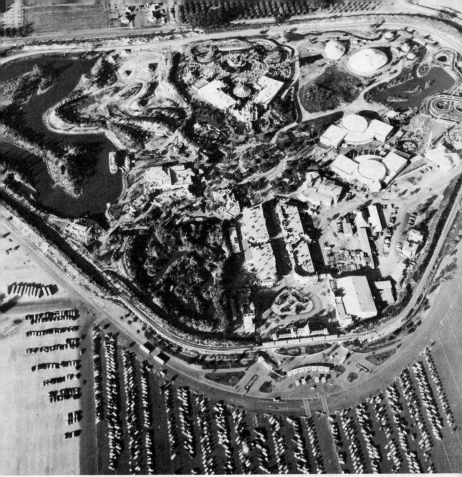

Disneyland from the air: On left are Adventureland and Frontierland, at top center is Fantasyland and on the right, Tomorrowland. Entrance is at bottom.

Frontierland revives America's past in a busy transportation center of early days.

"Mark Twain" is authentically re-created paddle wheeler that carries 300 people.

7

What's New in the U.S.A.

Luxurious new hotels are blossoming forth from the Atlantic to the Pacific. At top right is the new Fontainebleau, which adds still more glamor to Miami Beach.

In the Los Angeles area, the new Beverly Hilton features rooms with balconies.

Among the new ski facilities are double chair lifts at the Ski Bowl, Reno, Nevada.

Photos: Chris Hansen, Miami Beach News Bureau; Eddie Hoff, Beverly Hilton; Sierra Press Bureau

NEW ENGLAND

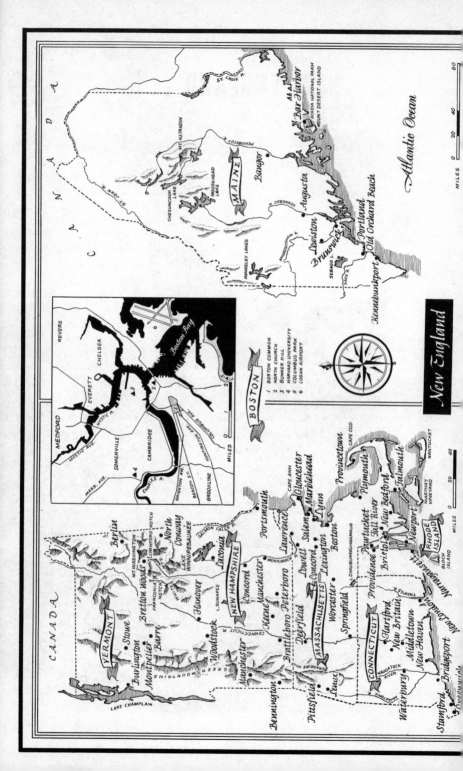

New England

COME "DOWN EAST" TO MAINE'S LAKES, WOODS AND SHORES

Pemaquid Light is at the tip of one of the many points that jut into the ocean north of Portland. Established 1827, it warned clipper ships of rocky peninsula.

Maine

New Harbor is fishing village and resort three miles from Pemaquid Point. It was home of Samoset, the Indian who startle the Pilgrims at Plymouth with his welcome

Maine's rolling slopes and the consistency of its snows make for ideal ski country.

Henry Wadsworth Longfellow taught a Bowdoin College. This is the Chapel

Photos: Grant M. Haist; Konstantin Kostich; Stephen Merril

cadia National Park is on Mount Desert land which also includes Bar Harbor.

Nearly cut in half by a fjord, with many hills and lakes, the island is beautiful.

Rockland and Camden on Penobscot Bay, re home ports for windjammer cruises.

"Alice S. Wentworth" is one of sailing ships offering salt-water vacation trips.

This scene in Camden harbor is typical of many of Maine's bay and river harbors.

Early morning stillness made possible the perfect reflections in this Maine cove.

Photos: National Park Service; Alice S. Wentworth Cruises; Maine Development Commission; Grant M. Haist

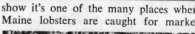

Pleasant Point is up near Passamaquoddy Bay, on the Canadian border. Lobster pots show it's one of the many places wher Maine lobsters are caught for marke

Lakes near Bridgton, 35 miles northwest of Portland, are good for trout and bass.

The Rangeley Lakes have such lovel names: Mooselookmeguntic, Umbago

Photos: Maine Development Commission; Kor stantin Kostich; Alfred E. Reichenberge

GREAT WHITE HILLS, LOVELY LAKES BECKON TO NEW HAMPSHIRE

he Old Man of the Mountain stands ard at Franconia Notch, scenic defile in the White Mountains. There is an aerial tramway and the famous Flume is nearby.

New Hampshire

Concord has been the capital since 1808; imposing State House was built in 1819.

Mt. Washington Cog Railway, completed in 1869, was first of its kind in the world.

Boyhood home of Franklin Pierce, 14th President of U.S., is in Hillsborough.

Skimobile Tramway at Mt. Cranmor near North Conway, carries passenge

Dartmouth College, founded 1769, is on of country's most distinguished liber

Berlin's 80-meter ski jump has highest steel ski tower (171½ ft.) in the U.S.

nearly a mile, with vertical lift of 1300 ft. It's used by skiers, summer sight-seers.

The White Island lighthouse, Isles of Shoals, lies off the coast near Portsmouth.

arts colleges for men. Dartmouth Winter Carnival is big social event at Hanover.

The Balsams, at Dixville Notch, is Swiss-like hotel on sparkling Lake Gloriette.

Photos: Eric M. Sanford; Cranmore Skimobile, Inc.; Dartmouth College News Service; Berlin Chamber of Commerce; Douglas Armsden; The Balsams

New Hampshire

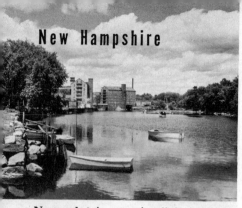

Newmarket is attractive little industrial community on shores of the Lamprey.

Village of Walpole has distinguished Unitarian Church, many lovely old homes.

New Hampshire granite has been used to fashion many U.S. buildings, monuments.

John Goffe's Mill, made famous by recent best seller, attracts many art students.

Visitors enter Hall of Ships at Lost River Reservation, near North Woodstock.

Chair lift at Mt. Sunapee State Park offers summer visitors a superb view.

18

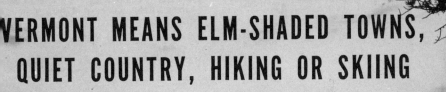

VERMONT MEANS ELM-SHADED TOWNS, QUIET COUNTRY, HIKING OR SKIING

Lake Champlain at sunset is typical of the peaceful scenes to be found in the Green Mountain State. This tremendous lake borders western Vermont for 100 miles.

19

Vermont

Playhouse at Weston is a fine 100-year-old structure that was formerly a church.

Ethan Allen, colonel of "Green Mountain Boys," stands at State House, Montpelier.

Half a hundred centers have been built up to accommodate winter sports fans in

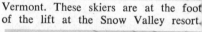

Vermont. These skiers are at the foot of the lift at the Snow Valley resort.

Derrick hoists granite block at Rock of Ages quarry, Barre, world's granite center.

Famous "Round Church" at Richmond is actually 16-sided. It was built in 1812.

Basin Harbor Club, Vergennes, is one of delightful resort areas along shore of Lake Champlain. This air view shows the Adirondacks across the lake in New York.

Hikers arrive to spend night at one of bunk houses on the 261-mile Long Trail.

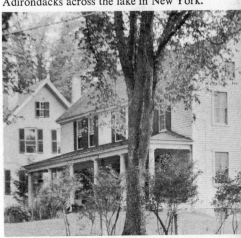

State constitution was adopted here at Old Constitution House, Windsor, in 1777.

Vermont

Bay Psalm Book was printed on this press, now at Historical Museum, Montpelier.

Hazen Road Monument at East Hardwic commemorates military road built in 1779

Historical Museum at Bennington ha relics, documents, utensils of early days

Mt. Mansfield, 4,393 ft. high, is summit of the Green Mountains. This area, near Stowe, is world renowned as winter sport center and also as summer vacationland.

Photos: Vermont Development Commission

IN MASSACHUSETTS
YOU RE-LIVE THE
BIRTH OF AMERICA

Bunker Hill monument on Breed's Hill, Charlestown, commemorates the stand of raw American militia against the cream of British troops, at start of Revolution.

23

Old South Meeting House shares with Faneuil Hall momentous oratory of 1770's.

Faneuil Hall, scene of important protest meetings, is called "Cradle of Liberty."

Paul Revere statue stands near the Old North Church, where the lanterns hung.

Blooming magnolias indicate that Spring has come to Commonwealth Avenue.

Iron grillwork distinguishes old houses on Beacon Street, opposite Boston Common.

Old waterfront, once host to ships from all over world, now has mostly fishing boats.

Photos: Massachusetts Department of Commerce; center right, TWA Trans World Airlines; bottom right, Konstantin Kostich

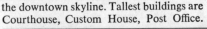

om **Memorial Drive in Cambridge,** you
k across the Charles River Basin to
the downtown skyline. Tallest buildings are
Courthouse, Custom House, Post Office.

gassiz House is recreation building at
dcliffe College for women, Cambridge.

Sightseeing boat on Charles passes one
of Harvard's dormitories, Dunster Hall.

blic Garden, with its celebrated swan
oats, has been treasured feature of city
for generations, as has also the Common
where free speech is honored every day.

Massachusetts

Old Deerfield is known for its historic houses. This is room of "Indian House."

Nearby Conway has beautifully simple house with a "ballroom" on second flo

Berkshire Music Festival is annual series of public concerts at Tanglewood estate in Stockbridge. Famous conductors dr music lovers from all of North Ameri

Farm house kitchen at Old Sturbridge village shows early American methods.

House of the Seven Gables, in Salem, said. to be setting of Hawthorne's nov«

Photos: Alfred E. Reichenberger, center and bott right; A. Milton Runyon, top right; Pioneer Val Association, top left; Old Sturbridge Villo

. **Greylock,** some 3,500 feet, is tallest the Berkshire Hills and highest mountain in the state. In winter dress, or autumn colors, it has majestic beauty.

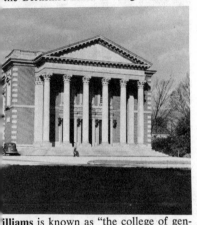

illiams is known as "the college of gentlemen." This is Chapin Hall auditorium.

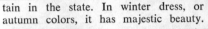

"Sweetheart Gate" is revered fixture of Mohawk Trail curio shop, Charlemont.

overed bridges are a New England feature that may disappear before onslaught of wide new roads. This fine example spans the Deerfield River near Charlemont.

otos: Mohawk Trail Association; center
t, Massachusetts Department of Commerce; bottom, Pioneer Valley Association

27

Massachusetts

Gloucester fishermen unload cod at this port with 300-year seafaring tradition.

Hadley's First Congregational Church h spire designed by Christopher Wre

This view of Connecticut River valley from Mt. Sugarloaf is typical of lovely farm country around South Deerfield an Sunderland, part of the "Pioneer Valley

Photos: Konstantin Kostich, t left; Pioneer Valley Associati

...mouth Rock, one of America's most ...ered shrines, is protected by imposing granite portico of classical design. It is visited by some half million annually.

...ck itself bears 1620 date as reminder ... year Pilgrims used this stepping-stone.

Each May traditional corn-planting is re-enacted at the Old Fort-Harlow House.

...hree famous statues: "Hail to the Sun-...se" greets visitors to Mohawk Trail.

Kitson's "Minuteman" stands on green at Lexington, the one by French at Concord.

Giant blue fin tuna, weighing 300 to 600 pounds. are landed at a Cape Cod harbor.

Cape Cod's 300 miles of coast pro scores of safe bays, inlets for sai

Provincetown's narrow streets and lanes delight visitors to its famous art colony.

Sandwich Congregational Church: Fam colored Sandwich glass was made in to

Photos: Cape Cod Chamber of Commerce; tom left, Massachusetts Department of Comm

esting cranberries: The September scape is brilliant with the crimson bogs and the colorful costumes of the berry pickers, some of Indian descent.

ody Tent at Hyannis presents operetta, ical comedy in theater-in-round style.

ked rug exhibition shows present-day les of favorite early American art.

Stoney Brook Mill at Brewster is first water power grist mill in the country.

Nantucket Island (25 mi. off Cape Cod) once was the great whaling port of world.

Jethro Coffin house, genuine "salt b style, is oldest on island, built 16

Old Mill on Nantucket has spar so fixed that vanes will turn only for West wind.

Martha's Vineyard is triangular isle elbow of Cape Cod. This is Edgarto

Gay Head Cliffs on Martha's Vineyard are noted for brilliant colors, especially when

reflected by the late afternoon sun. Wa panoag Indians make souvenirs of cl

Photos: Massachusetts partment of Comme top right by Eric M. San

Newport's famous 3-mile Cliff Walk along the Atlantic Ocean passes many fabulous summer residences built by millionaires. At left is Vanderbilt's "The Breakers."

Slater Park in Pawtucket has 193 acres of winding drives, flower gardens, a lake, and lagoons with artificial islands which contain the noted Shakespearean Garden.

State House overlooks busy Providence. It has world's second largest marble dome.

Craftsman at Gorham Company works on an exquisite sterling silver tea service.

At Brown's University Hall, French and U.S. troops were housed in Revolution.

Green Hall at University of Rhode Island houses library and administrative offices.

n Brown House, built 1786, is now the
dquarters of R. I. Historical Society.

Samuel Slater built first textile mill in
America on this Pawtucket site in 1790.

aval War College at Newport teaches
ficers, logistics to advanced tactics.

Huge yachts line up at Newport for start
of race to Bermuda, a sailing classic.

Rhode Island

All-steel Motor Vessel "Viking" takes to water at Blount Marine Works, Warren.

Block Island, fishing center and reso is 12 miles off the Rhode Island coa

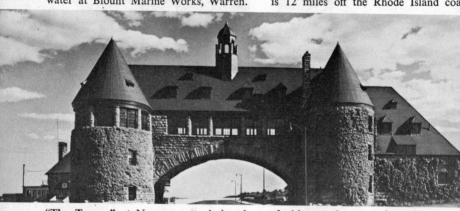

"The Towers" at Narragansett, designed by Stanford White, has been a landmark of this noted resort since the turn the century. It was originally a casin

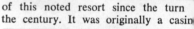

Old Colony House, Newport, is considered one of nation's best Colonial buildings.

Newport's Old Stone Mill was probab windmill, but legend calls it Norse reli

Photos: Rhode Islar
Development Counc

ld Lyme, where "a sea captain once ved in every house," is an elm-shaded village that typifies Connecticut. Present Congregational Church copies 1816 one.

Connecticut

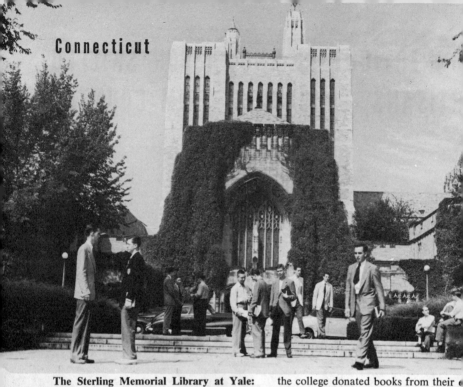

The Sterling Memorial Library at Yale: According to tradition, the founders of the college donated books from their libraries to start the school in 17

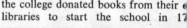

U.S. Naval Submarine Base, New London, operates "submarine escape training tank."

Choate School, exclusive prep school boys, has 500-acre campus at Wallingfor

Photos: Connecticut Development Commission; Offic
United States Navy Photograph; The Choate Sch

Corps of Cadets of the United States Coast Guard Academy, New London, lines up for review on the parade ground. Academy is "Annapolis" of Coast Guard.

Cadet Training Ship "Eagle" is part of floating equipment of $2,500,000 school.

Stanton House in Clinton is one of the many historic early homes in Connecticut.

Home office of the Aetna Life Affiliated Companies in Hartford is the largest colonial-style office building in the world. It's one-eighth of a mile long.

Photos: U. S. Coast Guard Academy; Connecticut Development Commission; Aetna Life Affiliated Companies

Connecticut

Intricate work of skilled craftsmen is shown at U. S. Time plant in Middlebury.

Stonington lighthouse, now a museum stood up under bombardment by Britis

Nathaniel Allis House, at Madison, is kept as in old days. This is the kitchen.

The Barnum Museum, Bridgeport, honors founder of Greatest Show on Earth

Clock Tower at Waterbury was modeled after the Torre del Mangia, Siena, Italy.

Gillette Castle, Hadlyme, is perched on cliff like medieval strongholds it copies

40

Mystic Seaport is 19th century coastal village being recreated by the Marine Historical Association. At left is the *Charles W. Morgan,* Yankee whaleship.

Pratt & Whitney Aircraft plant at East Hartford shows state's industrial power.

In 1851 the Sharps Company began making the famous Sharps rifles on this site.

Photos: Official Mystic Seaport Photo, Louis S. Martel; Pratt & Whitney Aircraft

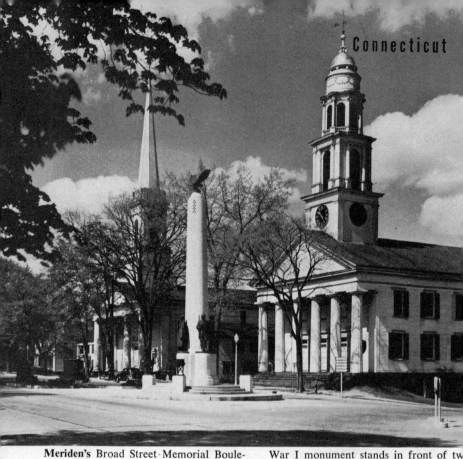

Meriden's Broad Street-Memorial Boulevard parallels the long Green. World War I monument stands in front of two churches, both over a hundred years old

The War Office at Lebanon was supply headquarters for Revolutionary troops.

Nathan Hale, of "I have but one life" fame, taught school here at East Haddam

Photos: Meriden Chamber of Commerce
Connecticut Development Commission

MID-ATLANTIC STATES

Photo: Surf fishing at Avon, New Jersey, by N. J. Department of Conservation and Economic Development

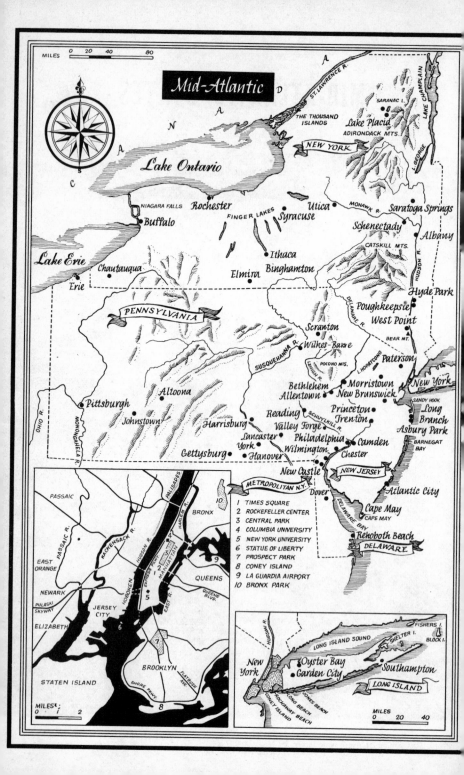

Mid-Atlantic

NEW YORK BOASTS THE WORLD'S LARGEST CITY AND GREATEST HARBOR

Looking south from 70th floor of RCA Building at dusk, you see lights aglow in Empire State Building (1472 ft. with television tower) and lower Manhattan.

Photo: Grant M. Haist

Bartholdi's Statue of Liberty welcomes ships as they arrive in New York harbor.

United Nations Secretariat Building has two sides entirely of glass, two of marble.

Ferry "Miss Liberty" carries half million visitors yearly from Battery to Statue.

Sightseeing yachts provide pleasant way of viewing all of Manhattan's skyline.

Sub-Treasury Building, Wall and Nassau streets, is of Greek Revival architecture.

Photos: New York State Department of Commerce; Trans World Airlines; Circle Line-Statue Ferry, Circle Line-Sightseeing Yachts, Inc.; Konstantin K

New York's City Hall has welcomed visitors from all over world for 150 years.

Heart of financial district, at lower tip of island, is seen from across river.

"The Bowery," famed in song and story, is a battered relic of its early days.

Photos: Konstantin Kostich; right, G. A. Reims

The "canyons" of the financial center are pictured at Pine Street and Broadway.

47

New York NEW YORK CITY

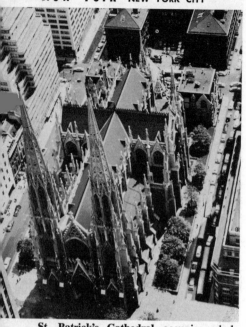

St. Patrick's Cathedral occupies whole block across from Rockefeller Center.

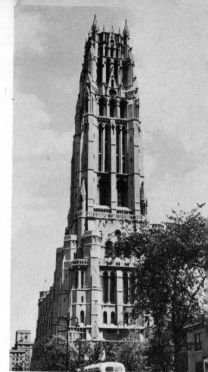

Riverside Church has impressive tower containing carillon of seventy-two bells.

Cathedral of St. John the Divine, when completed, will be the largest Gothic cathedral in the world. It has seven chapels clustered around soaring apse.

x

48

Photos: Konstantin Kostich

70-story RCA Building dominates 15-unit Rockefeller Center, "Radio City."

Looking east from RCA Building you see UN, East River, Grand Central, Chrysler.

Looking to south you see all of Lower Manhattan.

View to west from observation roof shows the *Queen Mary* in Hudson River, with New Jersey shore beyond.

In Lower Plaza is noted Prometheus Fountain.

Northward view pictures Central Park, lined on all sides with impressive apartment buildings, hotels, museums.

Photos: Rockefeller Center, Inc.; top right and lower left, Grant M. Haist; center left and lower right, Konstantin Kostich

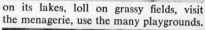

"Sunday in the Park" is favorite recreation of New Yorkers who boat or skate on its lakes, loll on grassy fields, visit the menagerie, use the many playgrounds.

Columbia University, founded in 1754 as Kings College, has over 22,000 students.

Hall of Fame at New York University honors American men and women of note.

Photos: G. A. Reims; bottom left, Konstantin Kostich

t Times Square, Broadway becomes the "Great White Way," aglow with hundreds of spectacular electric signs. Theaters make it the amusement center of nation.

erman Billingsley's Stork Club is one ' most famous night clubs in country.

Christmas brings enormous decorated tree to Rockefeller Plaza, songs by Choristers.

ack & Charlie's "21" always has autograph hunters waiting for celebrities.

Stage shows at Radio City Music Hall are famous for precision *Corps de Ballet.*

Brooklyn Bridge, built in 1883 by the Roeblings, was first to span East River.

George Washington Bridge, with Lincoln and Holland tunnels, cross Hudson River

Metropolitan Opera House is premier home of grand opera in the United States.

Washington Arch, at lower end of Fifth Avenue, is gateway to Greenwich Village

Chinatown is center for restaurants and curio shops, about 4,000 Chinese residents.

Grant's Tomb, Riverside Drive landmark honors Civil War general, 18th President

Photos: Northwest Orient Airlines: top right, center left, Konstantin Kostich United Air Lines; Grant M. Haist; New York State Department of Commerce

ney Island often attracts a million to its
ean beach, boardwalk and amusements.

lamas from Peru are among the curios
Bronx Zoo, one of world's largest.

arades up New York's great Fifth Ave-
ue honor holidays, heroes, special events.

Rockefeller Plaza outdoor ice skating
pond has twenty onlookers to each skater.

Japanese Garden, Rose and Rock Gardens
are found in Brooklyn Botanical Garden.

Sidewalk art shows encourage looking and
buying in bohemian Greenwich Village.

53

New York LONG ISLAND

Montauk Point is the eastern tip of Long Island. Its lighthouse, with black-and-

white-striped tower, was built in 1? Fishing grounds off the point are fam

Ducks on the hoof: Duck farms flourish along the many creeks of the South Shore.

Whalers Church at Sag Harbor lost spyglass-shaped tower in 1938 hurrica

Shelter Island nestles between the two eastern points of Long Island, Orient

Point on the north and Montauk to south, connected with both by ferr

54

Photos: top, Charles L. Sherman;
York State Department of Comm

nce an almost inaccessible sandbar, ones Beach is now state's best play spot.

Watertower, floodlighted at night and visible for 25 miles, dominates Jones Beach.

Sagamore Hill, recently opened to public, was home of Pres. Theodore Roosevelt.

Souvenirs of Rough Rider days, of big-game hunting, fill Teddy Roosevelt home.

Walt Whitman Birthplace in West Hills: Good Gray Poet was born here in 1819.

Country Life Press, Garden City, is one of world's great book publishing centers.

Photos: New York State Department of Commerce; bottom right, A. Milton Runyon

55

Franklin D. Roosevelt Library, at Hyde Park, houses six million of his papers.

Taylor Hall is at entrance to Vassar College for women, at Poughkeepsie.

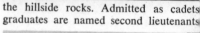

At West Point, the buildings of the U. S. Military Academy seem carved out of the hillside rocks. Admitted as cadets graduates are named second lieutenants

Harness racing at Goshen is climaxed by the internationally famous Hambletonian.

Mid-Hudson Bridge is at Poughkeepsie, half way between New York and Albany.

ear Mountain Bridge, about 40 miles
orth of New York, leads to Palisades

Interstate Park, with variety of sports
for New York-New Jersey residents.

Catskill Game Farm, in Greene County,
exhibits animals from all over the world.

Actors rehearse for summer theater at
Woodstock, widely known artist colony.

Tower in Catskills gives wide view. This
is noted as "Wish You Were Here" land.

Kayak sailing on Seventh Lake: There are hundreds of lakes in the Adirondacks.

Ausable Chasm is a wonderland of rock forms: Pulpit Rock, Devil's Oven, etc.

Schroon Lake is lovely 9-mile-long body of water that attracts many vacationists.

Legend says it was named after Madame de Maintenon, widow of Paul Scarron.

State operated bathing beach is one of many facilities of 33-mile Lake George.

Whiteface Mountain has elevator to lookout tower that gives a magnificent view.

Photos: New York State Department of Commerce; center, Konstantin Kostich

Saratoga Race Track, Saratoga Springs, is scene of internationally famous horse races during August, including the Travers and the Hopeful, test for two-year-olds.

Central Adirondacks offer winter sports thrills for youngsters and for grownups.

Snow tractor transports skiers in comfort at the Whiteface Mt. ski development.

Lake Placid ski jump: This village on Mirror Lake is famous as sport center.

Photos: New York State Department of Commerce; top, Henri Cartier-Bresson (Magnum)

Y-shaped Keuka Lake is the only one of the Finger Lakes with irregular outline.

About 19 miles long, it is noted for the many vineyards on the surrounding slopes.

The Krebs, Skaneateles, is one of most famous eating houses in upstate area.

Baseball Museum at Cooperstown reveres Abner Doubleday's invention of the sport.

McKinley Circle, Buffalo: This is the second largest city (580,000) in state.

Elmira was summer home of Mark Twain for many years. This is writer's studio.

Photos: New York State Department of Commerce; center left, A. G. Tarby

ailboats are towed to anchorage after a
ace on Cayuga Lake, largest of the six

Finger Lakes. Chief city on the lake is
Ithaca, the home of Cornell University.

Watkins Glen: The Gorge Trail is 2 miles
long, has some 700 steps, many bridges.

Taughannock Falls, 50 feet higher than
Niagara, is highest east of the Rockies.

Photos: Bill Ficklin; Alfred E. Reichenberger;
New York State Department of Commerce

The "Thousand Islands" actually number about 1700. About 20 of them are visible in this picture of the American channe of the St. Lawrence near Alexandria Bay

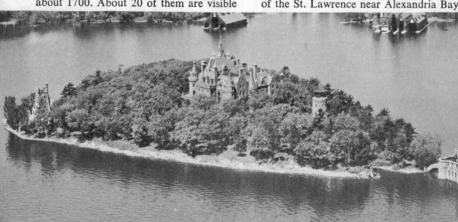

Boldt Castle was built on Heart Island by George C. Boldt, who rose from dish- washer to presidency of the company tha owned New York's Waldorf-Astoria hote**l**

...thouse on Cape Vincent: Many French ...ed here at time of Napoleon's exile.

Water tours visit the six state parks and view Thousand Island luxury estates.

...ernational highway, with several ...dges, crosses the St. Lawrence via Wells and Hill islands. It was opened in 1938. From mainland to mainland, it's 6 miles.

63

Niagara Falls is the largest cataract in
North America with total width of 4,750
feet. This is American Falls which
tered shape with recent erosion of r

Photo: Grant M. H

FIFTY MILLION A YEAR ENJOY
NEW JERSEY'S FAMOUS BEACHES

Atlantic City's fabulous boardwalk, immense hotels, Municipal Auditorium, Steel Pier all combine to make it one of world's most patronized year-round resorts.

Photo: New Jersey Department of Conservation and Economic Development.

New Jersey

Skyline of Trenton, New Jersey's capital, is dominated by dome of Statehouse.

This tall electric beacon marks Thomas A. Edison's workshop at Menlo Park.

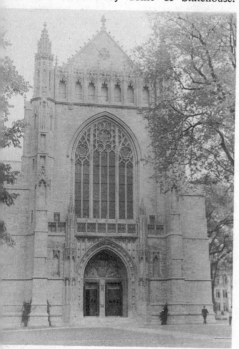

Princeton University Chapel ranks with Chicago and Cambridge as world's largest.

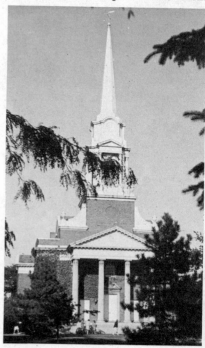

This is Voorhees Chapel of N. J. College for Women, a part of Rutgers University.

Photos: New Jersey Department of Conservation and Economic Development.

Asbury Park is best-known of the resorts along the northern part of New Jersey's coast. This is view of boardwalk looking north from Casino to Convention Hall.

Chalfonte-Haddon Hall is meeting-place of many of Atlantic City's conventions.

Cape May is at southernmost point of the state, between Delaware Bay and Atlantic.

Barnegat Lighthouse was replaced by lightship off-shore.

Manasquan and Brielle, on the Manasquan River where it flows into the Atlantic, are fishing headquarters.

Photos: Asbury Park Municipal Publicity Dept.;
Chalfonte-Haddon Hall; New Jersey Department
of Conservation and Economic Development.

New Jersey

George Washington slept here, at Wallace House, Somerville, near winter camp.

Walt Whitman lived in this modest Camden residence from 1884 until his death.

Alexander Hamilton monument, in a small park on the brink of the Palisades at Weehawken, marks spot of Burr-Hamilton duel. Across Hudson is New York skyline.

Basking Ridge oak, in Somerset County, has amazing branch spread of 140 feet.

Paulins Kill is one of many lakes and streams that provide good sport-fishing.

68

PENNSYLVANIA HAS HISTORIC SHRINES
FROM EARLY DAYS OF INDEPENDENCE

Philadelphia's Independence Hall, which houses Liberty Bell, witnessed the signing of the Declaration of Independence in 1776. Constitution was framed here, too.

Photo: TWA Trans World Airlines

Pennsylvania PHILADELPHIA

Franklin Institute has many exhibits, including Benjamin Franklin Printing Shop.

Liberty Bell developed crack in 1835 when tolling death of Chief Justice Marshall.

University of Pennsylvania was first in the country officially designated as such.

First Continental Congress assembled here in Carpenters' Hall on September 5, 1774.

Old Original Bookbinder's is a favorite restaurant, filled with mementoes of past.

Old Swedes Church, built in 1700, is the oldest church building in Philadelphia.

70

Betsy Ross House is reputed place where first American Flag was designed, sewn.

Wissahickon Valley, Walnut Lane Bridge show a pastoral section of Philadelphia.

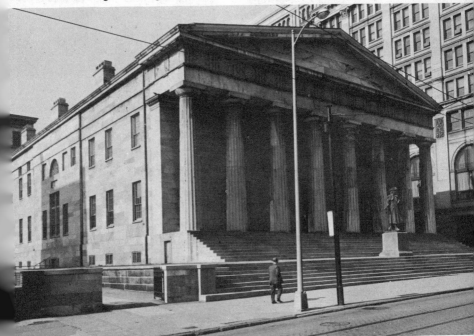

Old Custom House was originally home of the second Bank of the United States.

In front stands a statue of Robert Morris, a chief financier of American Revolution.

These soldiers' huts at Valley Forge are similar to those used by Washington's 11,000 ragged Continentals who camped here during crucial winter of 1777–1778.

Washington's Headquarters was scene of conferences with Lafayette, Knox, others.

Washington Memorial Carillon has 49 bells, one for each state, one for Union.

Photos: Pennsylvania State
Department of Commerce

Gettysburg was scene of three-day battle that marked turning point of Civil War.

Monument honors General Meade who led Union forces against General Lee's.

oldiers' National Cemetery has graves f 3,604 soldiers who died in battle be-

tween forces numbering 70,000 to 80,000 on each side. Cemetery covers 17 acres.

nnsylvania Memorial honors 34,530 en of state who took part in the battle.

National Monument is near spot where Abraham Lincoln gave Gettysburg speech.

Pennsylvania

Bucknell University, Lewisburg, is one of state's leading educational centers.

University of Pittsburgh's 42-story skyscraper is called "Cathedral of Learning."

Pittsburgh's "Golden Triangle" is area between Allegheny and Monongahela rivers.

One of the great steel centers of world is Pittsburgh's gigantic "Steel Valley."

Quaint buggies, homespun garb typify the Amish, one of state's many religious sects.

Hopewell Village, near Reading, has been re-created as it was in Revolutionary days.

74

Photos: Pennsylvania State Department of Commerce; to left, A. Milton Runyon; center left, Robert V. Pivirot

Delaware Water Gap Bridge spans river between New Jersey and Pennsylvania.

Capitol at Harrisburg was dedicated by President Theodore Roosevelt in 1906.

Cambria Inclined Plane connects Johnstown with Westmont, 504 feet higher.

Shaft commemorates Washington's crossing of Delaware in attack on Trenton.

Pennsylvania

U. S. Brig "Niagara" took decisive part in Battle of Lake Erie, during War of 1812.

Buck Hill Falls is hidden in deep gorge. Photo shows the Upper and Middle Falls.

The Inn at Buck Hill Falls in the Pocono Mountains was established in 1901 by a group of Philadelphia Quakers. It is on of America's prominent resort hotel

Horseshoe Curve of the Pennsylvania Railroad, constructed in 1852, is an out- standing engineering feat. The curve, wi 220-degree central angle, is 2,375 ft. lor

Photos: Pennsylvania State Department of Co merce; top right and center, Buck Hill Falls

DELAWARE IS PROUD OF ITS HISTORIC LANDMARKS

The County Court House at New Castle as served Delaware's government since the days of William Penn, making it oldest U. S. Court House in continuous use.

Photo: Delaware State evelopment Department

Delaware

First powder mill of E. I. duPont de Nemours used power of Brandywine Creek.

University of Delaware pioneered in Foreign Study, with exchange students.

Christ Church, Dover, possesses a Bible presented in 1767 by Benjamin Wynkoop.

Old State House, built in 1787, stands on the Green in Delaware's capital, Dover

Photos: Delaware State
Development Department

ehoboth Beach, largest summer resort
Delaware, occupies one of the few
spots along the South Atlantic coast where
the mainland extends right to surf's edge.

Wilmington is Delaware's one big city,
of 110,000 people. This is old City Hall.

Zwaanendael Museum, Lewes, commemorates settlement by the Dutch in 1631.

Delaware

Tourinns Motor Court, near Wilmington, is typical of modern highway facilities.

Old Swedes Church, built at Wilmington in 1698, has mementoes of many pioneers.

Old Drawyers Presbyterian Church dates from 1773. It is located near Appoquini-mink Creek, in Odessa. Many founders of the state are interred in its cemetery.

Photos: Delaware State Development Department; top left, Tourinns, Inc.

THE MIDSOUTH

Photo: Skyline Drive, Shenandoah National Park, by
Virginia Department of Conservation and Development

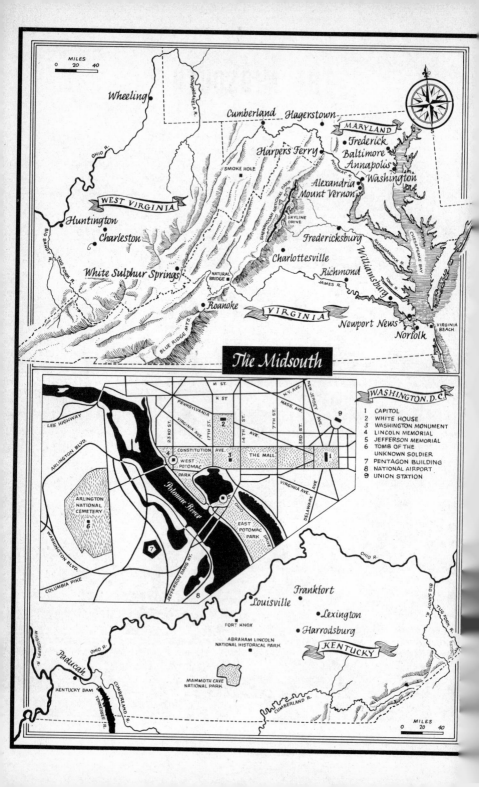

The Midsouth

WASHINGTON IS WORLD CITADEL OF FREEDOM

U. S. Capitol dominates Washington from summit of Capitol Hill. George Washington laid the cornerstone in 1793; statue of Freedom was placed atop dome in 1863.

Photo: Grant M. Haist

83

Washington, D.C.

Washington Monument, opened in 1888, is the world's tallest structure of masonry.

Air view of the Capitol shows its 120 acres of grounds. In the north wing, to

the left, is the Senate, and in the south
wing, the House of Representatives meets.
The building is 751 feet long, 350 wide,
and its dome rises to height of 285 feet.

Washington, D.C.

Visitors to the top of 555-ft. Washington Monument have a spectacular view of the city, and especially of the White House and its 18 acres of grounds. Every U.S

President has lived here since President John Adams moved to the unfinished building in 1800. It was completely rebuilt, within the original walls, in 1950–1952.

Photo: Grant M. Haist

Washington, D.C.

Arlington Memorial Bridge, built at cost of $10 million crosses Potomac from the Lincoln Memorial to Arlington National Cemetery. Photo shows end-of-day traffic.

Lincoln Memorial, built in general form of a Greek temple, is one of the world's most impressive memorials. 36 columns represent states at time of Presidency.

Photos: Grant M. Haist; Greater National Capital Committee

terior of Lincoln Memorial contains
gantic 19-ft. seated figure of Lincoln
by Daniel Chester French, in which the
artist has captured his brooding sadness.

oto: Grant M. Haist

Jefferson Memorial, completed in 1943, was dedicated on the 200th anniversary of the birth of Thomas Jefferson. I Pantheon design was one he often use

vering statue of Jefferson, the great
esman who wrote the Declaration of
Independence, is principal feature of the
Memorial. Quotations are carved on walls.

o: Grant M. Haist

National Gallery of Art is one of most famous in world. It was gift of Andrew W. Mellon. This view shows Constitutio Avenue entrance and the 7th Street sid

Rotunda in National Gallery has fountain surmounted by Giovanni Bologna's bronze Mercury. In famed collection are paintir by Stuart, Renoir, Vermeer, Hom

Photos: National Gallery of

tagon Building is across Potomac in ginia, but so much a part of life in Washington that we include it here. It's the largest office building in the world.

thsonian Institution houses amazing ntific exhibits, most popular being

The Spirit of St. Louis, the plane in which Lindbergh made solo flight to Paris.

os: Ewing Galloway;
ry of Congress

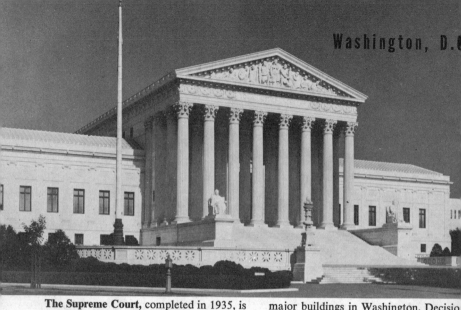

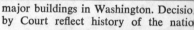

The Supreme Court, completed in 1935, is one of newest and most beautiful of the major buildings in Washington. Decisio by Court reflect history of the natio

Abraham Lincoln was fatally shot, here at Ford's Theater, by John Wilkes Booth.

Old Peterson House, where Lincoln di in April 1865, is across from theat

Occidental Restaurant is noted eating place next door to famous Willard Hotel.

Photographs of military men and oth celebrities line walls of the Occident

Photos: Library of Congr
bottom, Occidental Restaur

e **Third State House** to be built on same site in Annapolis, this one es back to 1772. It is the oldest state capitol in America still in daily use, and the only one in which the Congress of the United States has convened.

o: Maryland Department of Information

Maryland

"Tecumseh" is revered by midshipmen at United States Naval Academy, Annapolis.

Academy Chapel has crypt containin tomb of daring hero, John Paul Jone

St. John's College, Annapolis, was the first free school in original 13 colonies.

Annapolitans model fashions of ancest at historic Hammond-Harwood hou

Photos: Maryland Department of Informa

Ocean City is Maryland's only resort by the sea. Located on sandy strip between Sinepuxent Bay and the Atlantic, it has ocean and bay swimming, fishing, yachting.

Fort McHenry repulsed British in 1814; was birthplace of "Star Spangled Banner."

And battle-scarred Fort Frederick dates back to 1756, in days of the Indian wars.

Antietam Battlefield, near Hagerstown, was scene of one of the hardest-fought Civil War battles, on September 17, 1862. Markers show ebb and flow of fierce battle.

Maryland

Hagerstown, a manufacturing city, boasts Museum of Fine Arts, in a lovely setting.

The "Narrows," near Cumberland, was famous gateway to the west 200 years ago.

Fairchild Aircraft plant, near Hagerstown, is responsible for the city's nickname,

"The Home of the Flying Boxcars." Other plants make furniture, pipe organs, shoes.

Wye Oak is the state tree. Maryland has twelve extensive park and forest areas.

Princess Anne, one of the earliest settlements, has old homes like Teackle House

Photos: top left, Raup, Maryland Department of Information; top right, Cumberland Chamber of Commerce center, Maryland Department of Information; bottom M. E. Warren, Maryland Department of Information

VIRGINIA, "MOTHER OF PRESIDENTS,"
HAS WEALTH OF SCENERY, HISTORY

Photo: Court House, Charlottesville,
Henri Cartier-Bresson (Magnum)

Virginia WILLIAMSBURG

Williamsburg is delightful replica of our Colonial past. Magazine was built 1715.

In this 18th century Capitol, Patrick Henry made speech against the Stamp Act

Raleigh Tavern has been refurnished according to inventories of early keeper

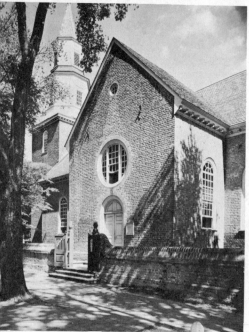

Bruton Parish Church has been restored to its appearance when built in 1710–15.

Public Gaol: Minor offenders were punished in the stocks and pillory in front

Photos: Colonial Williamsburg; top right, Konstantin Kost

overnor's Palace, considered one of the ndsomest estates in colonial America, was the official residence of the king's representative in the Virginia Colony.

illiamsburg Inn, just outside restored ea, has fine facilities for visitors.

Early costumes recreate lavishness of colonial life under the British crown.

otos: Colonial Williamsburg; bottom right, Vir-
nia Department of Conservation and Development

101

Virginia

Skyline Drive is 107 miles long, from Front Royal on the north to Rockfish Gap near Waynesboro on the south. The it links up with the Blue Ridge Parkwa

Shenandoah National Park is 300-square-mile tract of mountains and ridges that extends on either side of the Skyli Drive. It has 200 miles of hiking trai

Photos: Virginia Department of Conservation and Developm

The Homestead, at Hot Springs, is one of the world's famous hotels. First inn on the site dates from 1765. The modern building radiates from 12-story tower.

James Monroe, as a young attorney, used his modest Law Office, Fredericksburg.

University of Virginia was founded 1819 by Thomas Jefferson. This is the Rotunda.

James Monroe built Oak Hill, near Aldie, during his first term as President. He spent much time here, making journeys to and from the Capital on horseback.

Virginia

Monticello, the home of Thomas Jefferson, was designed and built by the statesman himself. He died here on July 4, 1826, fiftieth anniversary of Independence Day.

Luray Caverns, beneath western slopes of Blue Ridge, have great underground halls.

Shenandoah is another of Virginia's nine caverns. This is the Grotto of the Gods.

Photos: Virginia Department of Conservation and Development

Here at Mount Vernon, plantation home overlooking the Potomac River, George Washington lived the life he loved best —that of a prosperous country squire.

Stonewall Jackson taught at "V.M.I."— Virginia Military Institute, Lexington.

Natural Bridge, 215 feet high, is one of the seven natural wonders of the world.

Virginia

State Capitol at Richmond is one of many buildings designed by Thomas Jefferson.

It contains Houdon statue of Washington only one of the President made from life

Westover, home of the famous Byrd family of Virginia, is along the James River.

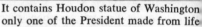

Kenmore was home of Washington's sister Betty, and her husband, Colonel Lewis

Girls from Mary Washington College serv tea in the stately dining room at Kenmor

106

Photos: Virginia Department Conservation and Developme

Valentine Museum, Richmond, houses work of sculptor Edward V. Valentine.

White House of Confederacy, at Richmond, was the home of Jefferson Davis.

Stratford was birthplace of the Lees of Virginia, including the famous Robert E.

"Mother's Room" at Stratford: The great plantation, now restored, borders Potomac.

This is gracious dining room of house in which George Washington was born, 1732.

Exterior of Birthplace: Rebuilt like the original, it is now a National Monument.

Photos: Virginia Department of Conservation and Development; bottom right, U. S. Department of the Interior

107

Arlington House, in Arlington National Cemetery, was built by step-grandson of George Washington. Robert E. Lee was married here, lived in house until 1861.

Woodrow Wilson was born in this square house at Staunton, on December 28, 1856.

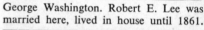

Presbyterian Meeting House, Alexandria: Unknown Soldier of Revolution lies here.

Gunston Hall was home of George Mason, outstanding author of the Bill of Rights.

St. Luke's Church, near Smithfield, is one of nation's oldest, built in 1632.

Photos: Virginia Department of Conservation and Development

Shirley, one of the largest of Tidewater Virginia mansions, was built between 1720 and 1740 by Thomas West and his three brothers. Lawn slopes to James River.

James Monroe built Ash Lawn near Monticello, so he could be near his friend and mentor, Thomas Jefferson. Estate is known for its beautiful boxwood hedges.

Photos: Virginia Department of Conservation and Development

Virginia

Old church tower, Jamestown: This was site of first permanent English settlement.

St. John's Church, Richmond, echoed to Patrick Henry's cry for "liberty or death."

Virginia Beach, on the Atlantic near Norfolk, is an outstanding shore resort.

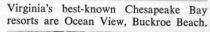

Virginia's best-known Chesapeake Bay resorts are Ocean View, Buckroe Beach.

George Washington Masonic National Memorial Temple towers over Alexandria.

Boyhood home of Patrick Henry, this old house became Michie Tavern in 1746.

110

Photos: Virginia Department of Conservation and Development; bottom right, Michie Tavern

WHITE SULPHUR IS NOTED RESORT OF "MOUNTAIN STATE," WEST VIRGINIA

The original White Sulphur Springs Hotel was renowned for more than half a century as the Old White. Belle, in front of Greenbrier, re-creates ante-bellum days.

Photo. Greenbrier News Bureau

West Virginia

Woodburn Hall is symbol of West Virginia University, situated at Morgantown.

West Virginia's State Capitol is located at Charleston, in Appalachian foothills.

Greenbrier College for Women, originally Lewisburg Seminary, was founded in 1812.

Harewood, in Eastern Panhandle, was built by Washington for his brother, Samuel.

"Old Stone Face" gazes across creek at Beckwith Cut-Off, near Chimney Corner.

112

Hawks Nest State Park provides breathtaking view of the New River Gorge, east of Charleston. The towering rock is named for the fish hawks that once nested there.

At Blackwater Falls, the dark hued river drops over broken ledge to huge boulders.

Smoke Hole Cavern was used by Indians and early white settlers to cure meats.

Monument above and "John Brown's Fort" at right commemorate the stand which the famed abolitionist made against force of marines prior to start of the Civil War.

Indian Burial Mound, in Staunton Park at South Charleston, is 175 feet around at base and 30 feet high. Many Indian ornaments, stone weapons have been found.

The Castle, Berkeley Springs, was built by Judge Soult as a "castle in the air."

Carbide and Carbon Chemicals Corporation is one of state's many industrial plants.

114

KENTUCKY IS A LAND OF BLUEGRASS, RACE HORSES, AND GRACIOUS LIVING

Horse farm region of Kentucky centers round Lexington. Visitors may see the thoroughbreds that have made history and watch gambols of promising young colts.

Kentucky

Bluegrass name comes from steel-blue tint of May blossoms. It's ideal for grazing.

Capitol, built in 1909, is at Frankfort in center of state, along Kentucky River.

Mammoth Cave covers an area ten miles in circumference and has 325 explored passageways which extend 150 miles. This is Crystal Lake, an outstanding feature

116

Churchill Downs in Louisville is scene of America's most celebrated horse race, the Kentucky Derby. More than 100,000 fans gather here first Saturday in May.

Air view of Calumet Farm shows beautiful barns, outdoor track, miles of rolling blue- grass where many thoroughbred winners have been raised. It covers 1,000 acres.

Kentucky

Kentucky Dam is major TVA dam, finished 1944, 206 ft. high, 8,422 ft. long.

Kentucky Lake, formed by dam, is sport center with three state parks on shores.

Laurel Cove, Pine Mountain State Park, is scene of the annual Mountain Laurel

Festival. High point of 3-day event is crowning of the queen by the Governor.

Liberty Hall, in Frankfort, was home of John Brown, state's first U.S. Senator.

Diamond Point is one of Harrodsburg' old homes in southern plantation style

118

Photos: top left, Robert H. Fait
Kentucky Division of Publici

This memorial honors the birthplace of Abraham Lincoln, near Hodgenville, in central Kentucky. The birth cabin is preserved inside the memorial building.

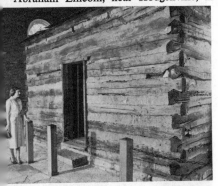

Log house where Lincoln's parents were married stands at Pioneer Memorial Park.

Split-rail fence appropriately marks boundaries at Lincoln Memorial Park.

Marriage Temple shelters cabin where Thomas Lincoln married Nancy Hanks.

At Federal Hill, near Bardstown, Stephen Foster wrote "My Old Kentucky Home."

Kentucky

Restored buildings at old Fort Harrod are furnished in manner of pioneer days.

Fine burley tobacco is grown in bluegrass section and taken to market at Lexington.

Monument to Jefferson Davis, President of the Confederacy, stands at Fairview.

Boone Tavern at Berea is operated by Berea College as a student industry.

Graves of Daniel and Rebecca Boone are on a high bluff in Frankfort cemetery.

Photos: Kentucky Division of Publicity

THE SOUTH

Photo: Sanibel Island, Florida,
by Florida State News Bureau

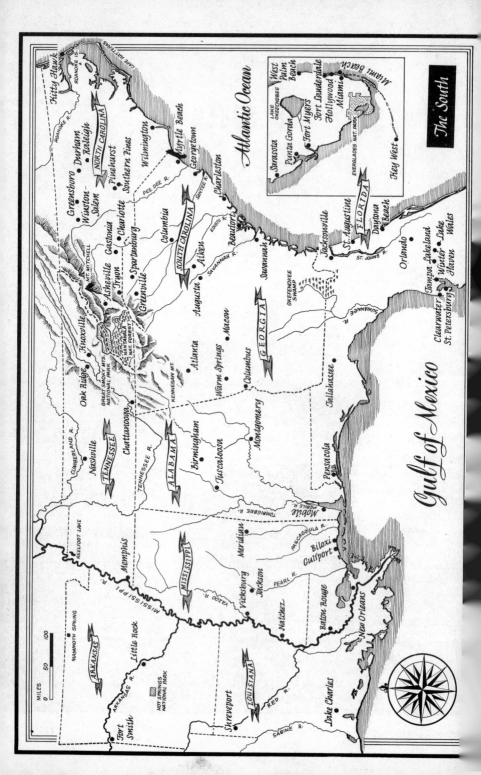
The South

FROM HATTERAS TO GREAT SMOKIES, NORTH CAROLINA OFFERS INFINITE VARIETY

Great Smoky Mountains National Park is shared by North Carolina, Tennessee.

The "Great Smokies" take their name from bluish perpetual haze found here.

Photo: National Park Service

Mile-High Overlook is on new section of the Blue Ridge Parkway, extending from Soco Gap to Black Camp Gap at boundary of Great Smokies Nat'l Park.

Chimney Rock, Eastern America's greatest monolith, rises 315 feet from its base.

Old Market House, built 1838, stands "where all roads meet" in Fayetteville.

124

Photos: North Carolina News Bureau, top by Gus Martin; bottom left, Delta-C&S Air Lines

Near Asheville, the mountain-top Craggy Gardens may be seen from Blue Ridge Parkway. In late May and June, acres of rhododendrons bloom in a blaze of color.

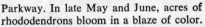

Old Well, in classic little temple, is landmark of University of North Carolina.

Floodlighted, North Carolina's Capitol stands out from surrounding oak grove.

North Carolina State Fair Arena, five miles west of Raleigh, is one of the most remarkable buildings ever constructed. It has seating capacity of more than 9,000.

Mount Mitchell, in western part of state, is 6,684 feet—the highest in Eastern America. State park on the summit may be reached by five-mile paved highway.

Home Moravian Church is one of historic buildings in industrial Winston-Salem.

A million azaleas greet early spring in Wilmington at many garden plantations

Photos: North Carolina News Bureau, top and left
by Gus Martin, bottom right by Hugh Morton

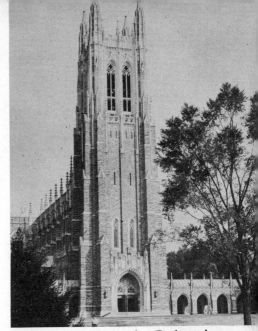

Wright Brothers National Memorial, near Kitty Hawk, marks birth of powered flight.

Chapel at Duke University, Durham, is beautiful example of Gothic architecture.

Pisgah National Forest is million-acre tract in western part of state, parts of which may be reached by motor roads. This is trail beside river at North Mills.

Photos: North Carolina News Bureau; bottom, U. S. Forest Service

Nantahala National Forest is another million-acre tract, known as "Land of the Noonday Sun," in southwestern part of state. This is the Nantahala gorge.

Tobacco production in state is valued at over $460 million. This is auction room.

Principal cigarette factories are located at Durham, Reidsville and Winston-Salem

Biltmore House, near Asheville, was George Vanderbilt estate, built in 1890.

Governor's Mansion, Raleigh, is Quee Anne style. Furnishings are magnificen

Photos: U. S. Forest Service; North Caro lina News Bureau, center left by Sebastie Sommer, bottom right by Gus Mart

LOVELY OLD GARDENS ARE MEMORABLE
FEATURE OF SOUTH CAROLINA

The great gardens of South Carolina lure thousands of visitors each spring. Among the principal ones are Magnolia, Cypress, Middleton (above), and Brookgreen.

Photo: Konstantin Kostich

Fort Sumter, in Charleston Harbor, was scene of first shot fired in Civil War.

Charleston's Dock Street Theater was formerly the famous Old Planters Hotel.

Stuart House, with arched entrance and fluted columns, is beautiful old home.

Lofty octagonal steeple of St. Philip's Episcopal Church is Charleston landmark.

Miles Brewton House is most elegant example of Charleston Georgian residence

Photos: Charleston Chamber of Commerce; top left by Ronald A. Reilly, others by Alm Crenshaw; top right, Delta-C&S Air Line

Many great estates like Bonny Hall were built on rice plantations. The tidewater cultivation of rice, with elaborate dikes and canals, once produced half U.S. crop.

Inky waters of Cypress Gardens reflect the great trees and brilliant azaleas. Visitors may view the gardens, open from Thanksgiving to May 1, from little boats.

Photos: A. Milton Runyon; South Carolina State Development Board, Columbia

South Carolina

Aiken, in the west central sandhills, is known as the "Polo Capital" of the South.

State House at Columbia was bombed by General Sherman while it was being built.

Library at University of South Carolina was first separate library by U.S. college.

Marine base at Parris Island, Beaufort has trained thousands of U. S. Marines

Crofut House is one of many old homes that give Beaufort an Old World charm.

Four former rice plantations were joine to form 4,000-acre Brookgreen Garden

132

GRACIOUS GEORGIA HAS VARIED TOPOGRAPHY, VARIED INTERESTS

Savannah River, 314 miles long, forms the boundary between Georgia, South Caro- lina. Nicknamed "Cracker State," Georgia is the largest state east of the Mississippi.

Photo: Southern Photo Service, Inc., Georgia Department of Commerce

Atlanta, state capital and largest city, is called the "Gateway to the South." Capitol is at right, city hall left, an[d] Peachtree Street shopping center at to[p]

Cyclorama depicts Battle of Atlanta, at start of Sherman's "March to the Sea."

Municipal Auditorium in Hurt Park: A[t]lanta has many colleges and universitie[s]

Photos: Delta-C&S Air Lin[e]
Georgia Department of Commer[ce]
lower left by Carolyn Car[ter]

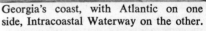

The Cloister is famous resort on Sea Island, one of the "Golden Isles" off Georgia's coast, with Atlantic on one side, Intracoastal Waterway on the other.

Okefenokee Swamp covers 700 square miles, is nation's most famous, primitive.

National cemetery at Marietta is burial place of 3,000 soldiers of Confederacy.

Savannah, Georgia's oldest city, is port of entry, industrial and shipping center.

Independent Presbyterian Church is one of proud buildings in tree-shaded Savannah.

Old stone wall leading to water: Savannah was once busiest port in the whole South.

Monterey Square is one of more than 5 parks that dapple the city with gree

Air view of Savannah, looking east, with Savannah River at the left: City is 17 miles from river's mouth on the Atlantic. Mild climate attracts many winter visitors.

The Old Pink House dates from 1771, way back in Savannah's days of crinolines.

Herb House, built as tool shed in 1734, considered oldest building in state.

Cotton merchants once made big fortunes in these historic houses on Bay Street.

Photos: Chamber of Commerce of Savannah; center right, Southern Photo Service, Inc., bottom right, Gabriel Benzur—Georgia Department of Commerce

Georgia

Fort Pulaski, on Cockspur Island, is named for hero of the Revolutionary War.

Iron lacework decorates porch of Juliette Low house, one of ante-bellum homes.

Warm Springs Foundation, for polio aid, was established by Franklin D. Roosevelt.

Ocmulgee National Monument, near Macon, has museum run by Park Service

Henry W. Grady, journalist and orator, lived in this stately mansion at Athens.

Grove Point is one of great plantatior reminiscent of Gone with the Wind's Tar

138

FLORIDA ENJOYS 1,200-MILE COAST, YEAR-ROUND MILD CLIMATE

Sun, sand, surf and wind-swept palms have attracted millions of visitors to Florida's coasts, both Atlantic and Gulf. This is Delray Beach, near Lake Worth.

Photo: Charles L. Sherman

Miami's Crandon Park beach boasts miles of wide, white ocean sand. The "Gold Coast," from Miami north to Hobe Sound, is nearest thing to an America Riviera.

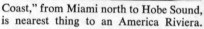

Horses round the first turn at Gulfstream one of three tracks in Greater Miami area

Dade County Courthouse, downtown Miami, is tallest building south of Baltimore.

Miami International Airport is traffi center for West Indies, South America

Photos: City of Miami News Burea bottom right, Delta-C&S Air Line

Miami Beach's fabled mile of gigantic hotels: Each has its own swimming pool and span of beach. Biscayne Bay causeways connect Miami Beach with Miami.

Orange Bowl has 65,000 capacity-crowd for annual New Year's Day football game.

Flagler Street and Biscayne Boulevard are at heart of Miami business section.

Miami skyline from across Biscayne Bay: The city's growth has been little short of miraculous. Little more than a village 50 years ago, population is now 250,000.

y

Photos: City of Miami News Bureau; top, Delta-C&S Air Lines

141

Jacksonville has 4 bridges over St. Johns River. Newest is Gilmore Street Bridge, foreground, opened to traffic in 1954. The city was named for Andrew Jackson.

Hemming Park is tropic oasis in midst of bustling Jacksonville business district.

Jacksonville's huge Union Terminal is junction point for East Coast, West Coast.

142

Photos: Charles Smith Studio; Marsh-Kornegay, Inc.; City of Jacksonville

Castillo de San Marcos, also called Fort Marion, is oldest fort standing in the U.S. Begun in 1672, but not finished until 1756, it is now National Monument.

St. Augustine's "Oldest House," now a museum, was reputedly built in 1500's.

This well is said to be Fountain of Youth that Ponce de Leon drank from in 1513.

Ponte Vedra Club is delightful resort five miles south of Jacksonville Beach.

Photos: Florida State News Bureau; Ponte Vedra Club

Florida EAST COAST

Daytona Beach is famed for hard-packed sand on which automobiles can be driven.

The 25-mile strip, 500 feet in width, h often been used for auto speed trial

Coral Sands cottages, at Ormond Beach, are typical of modern resort facilities.

Motorcycle races, too, have been he on the hard white sand of Daytona Beac

Marineland, just south of St. Augustine, is the world's largest oceanarium, with

leaping porpoises and other denizens sea in tremendous 700,000 gallon tan

144

Palm Beach is exclusive resort, on tip of 18-mile island between Lake Worth and the Atlantic. It ranks with Newport as vacation center for the socially elite.

McKee Jungle Gardens, just south of Vero beach, have 80 acres of luxuriant tropical plants, with thousands of orchids and other exotic flowers, trees, shrubs.

Boca Raton Hotel and Club, once private club for millionaires, is now luxurious resort hotel. It's between Delray Beach and Fort Lauderdale, has own golf course

Hollywood Beach Trailer Park: Florida offers world's best facilities for trailers.

Hollywood is winter home of Riverside Academy, a preparatory military school

Palm-lined boardwalk at Hollywood Beach: This resort, south of Fort Lauderdale, was founded by a Californian, but bears no resemblance to movie capital

146

Photos: Richard B. Hoit; Florida State News Bureau; Walter Gray, Hollywood By-the-Sea

Mid-winter finds Fort Lauderdale Beach lined with hundreds of gay beach cabanas.

City has many natural waterways, 90 miles of canals, Port Everglades harbor.

Crowd lines Intracoastal Waterway for Fort Lauderdale water-skiing, boat races.

Sightseeing tours by boat leave for New River, Pan-American Park, Everglades.

Pleasure boat traffic on New River: Fort Lauderdale is called "Venice of America."

Fabulous Bahai-Mar yacht basin offers berths for 400 yachts and power cruisers.

University of Florida, at Gainesville, has upwards of 10,000 students enrolled.

Rollins College, Winter Park, has 600-acre campus on shore of Lake Virginia.

Singing Tower, near Lake Wales, memorial to Edward Bok, has 71-bell carillon.

More than a hundred ferns and related tropical plants are found in the state.

Air plants, small spiny growths, derive their sustenance entirely from the air.

148

Photos: Florida State News Bureau; U. of F. Division of Public Relations

Orlando, from across Lake Eola: Recent rapid growth has made it largest inland city in the state. Often called the "City Beautiful," it is year 'round playground.

Orlando's Lake Ivanhoe is large enough for sailboat racing. Orlando Yacht Club is on Lake Conway at Pine Castle. There are 44 lakes within Orlando city limits.

Orlando is citrus-fruit shipping center, with nurseries, packing houses, canneries.

Kissimmee, known locally as Cow Town, is one of the state's chief cattle areas.

Photos: Greater Orlando Chamber of Commerce; bottom, Florida State News Bureau

149

Silver Springs is said to be world's largest, with a flow of 500 to 800 million gallons daily. Photo-sub and glass-bottomed boats show fish, aquatic plants in the depths.

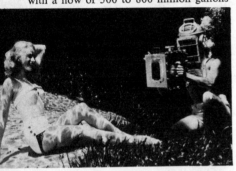

Underwater photograph of bathing beauty is stunt at fascinating Silver Springs.

Visitors watch, and take photos, through glass bottom of electrically-propelled boat.

Florida's tropical plants, such as this Alla-manda, bloom in summer, others in winter.

Bougainvillea is tropical plant that add color to landscape with brilliant flowers

Photos: Florida's Silver Spring bottom, Florida State News Burea

Cypress Gardens, near Winter Haven, attracts a quarter million visitors each year to its forested lagoons and acres of azaleas, camellias, hibiscus, bougainvillea.

You may see Cypress Gardens by boat, or wander along beautiful, landscaped paths.

Famous "aquamaids" perform daily ballet, often shown on newsreels of gardens.

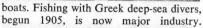

Tarpon Springs is one of largest sponge markets in world, with fleet of 70 or more boats. Fishing with Greek deep-sea divers, begun 1905, is now major industry.

Tallahassee, with its State Capitol, is attractively set among hills and lakes.

Silver-scaled tarpon make tremendous leaps as they battle fisherman in Gulf.

Clearwater Beach is on island in Gulf, connected by Memorial Causeway with the mainland. Clearwater itself is center for growing, shipping citrus fruits, gladioli.

DeSoto Oak, one of state's biggest, is at entrance to University of Tampa campus.

Latin-American Fiesta is annual event at Tampa, biggest port and industrial city.

2,400-ft. Municipal Pier is trademark of the "Sunshine City," St. Petersburg.

Many of St. Petersburg's 3,800 sidewalk benches are placed along Central Avenue.

Sailboats pass Vinoy Park hotel on way to a day of sport in sheltered Tampa Bay.

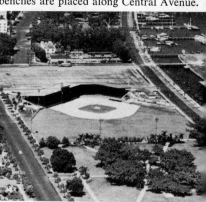

Al Lang Field: Two major league teams, Cards and Yankees, train at St. Pete.

New $22 million Sunshine Skyway extends 15 miles, St. Petersburg to Palmetto.

Spring Fiesta at St. Petersburg is 3-day frolic, with parades and Coronation Ball.

Jungle Gardens, just north of Sarasota, has thousands of native and imported trees, plants and shrubs in junglelike setting. It's outstanding tropical botanical garden.

Flamingoes, other rare birds, wade in the beautiful dark waters of Jungle Gardens.

Ringling Museum of Art at Sarasota has 700 old masters collected by showman.

Thomas A. Edison home at Fort Myers: The inventor came here 1886 for experiments with his incandescent lamp. Each February, Pageant of Light honors him.

"Money tree" in Edison garden: Over 60 kinds of tropical palms are found here.

Yacht basin: Fort Myers is situated on the mile-wide Caloosahatchee River.

Sanibel Island, in Gulf off Fort Myers, is noted for number, variety of sea shells

Everglades National Park is our newest, dedicated in June, 1947. It is 1¼ million acres of tropical scene, a wilderness of strange, exotic plant, bird, animal life.

After Seminole Wars, many Indians were removed to Oklahoma, but a number stayed in Everglades and Big Cypress. Above is Musa Isle Village, in Miami.

hotos: Florida State News Bureau; Kon-
tantin Kostich; City of Miami News Bureau

Key West is southernmost city in U.S. Fishing boats go after shrimp, turtles.

Lighthouse is known as only one in the country within corporate limits of a city.

Fort Jefferson, now a National Monument, is on Garden Key of the Dry Tortu-gas, 60 miles from Key West. It was from here that the *Maine* sailed for Havana.

Florida National Bank building shows the "different" appearance of Key West.

This home, with its Captain's Walk, is typical of the Bahamas-style residences.

Turtles, weighing up to 600 pounds, ar brought by fishermen to the soup plants

Photos: top left, Dr. Jacob
Klein; Florida State News Bureau

ALABAMA MEANS AZALEAS, COTTON, CATTLE, LUMBER

Bellingrath Gardens has fabulous collection of rare azaleas and camellias. It is a must on the itinerary of winter and spring visitors to Mobile's Azalea Trail.

Photo: Wm. Lavendar

Alabama

Statue of Vulcan, made for St. Louis Exposition, dominates hill near Birmingham.

Mardi Gras Carnival at Mobile, instituted in 1704, rivals the one at New Orleans.

Famous oak drive at Spring Hill College on the Mobile Azalea Trail: The annual flower festival is held in February or early March when azaleas are in full bloom.

160

Photos: Birmingham Chamber of Commerce; Official State of Alabama; Wm. Lavend

Birmingham, largest city in Alabama, is leading iron and steel center and is often called "Pittsburgh of the South." Downtown is laid out in planned squares.

First White House of the Confederacy was Montgomery home of Jefferson Davis.

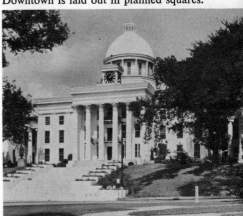

Timepiece above entrance to Capitol was the town clock of Montgomery until 1852.

Members of Azalea Trail "court" are shown during a visit to the Bellingrath Gardens. The trail begins in Mobile's Bienville Square, is well marked by signs.

Alabama

Alabama State Coliseum, Montgomery, is outstanding in its modern architecture.

Tuskeegee Monument honors the gre Negro educator, Booker T. Washingto

Helen Keller, who won out over deafness, blindness, was born here in Tuscumbia.

Rosemount is 20-room plantation mansic near Eutaw which took five years to buil

Gorgas House, with typical portico, is at University of Alabama, Tuscaloosa.

Cotton raising is still a major occupa tion, but hand-picking is on way ou

DEEP-SOUTH TRADITION IS STRONG
IN MAGNOLIA STATE OF MISSISSIPPI

Gloucester, open to visitors during the Natchez Pilgrimage, is oldest mansion in the district. It was home of Winthrop Sargent, the first Territorial governor.

Mississippi River at Vicksburg: A major river port, Vicksburg overlooks junction of Yazoo Canal and the Mississippi. It was known as "Gibraltar of Confederacy."

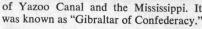

Dunleith is stately mansion, with tall Doric columns, on outskirts of Natchez.

This cypress swamp is on Natchez Trace, new Parkway following historic old road.

Iuka Mineral Springs were discovered by Indians, later became noted health resort.

MacArthur Hotel, Biloxi: This was first French settlement in Mississippi Valley.

164

Melrose is especially popular with visitors during the Pilgrimage because it is one of the best-preserved old homes, with furnishings much as in the 1840's.

Jefferson Military Academy, Washington, was scene of Aaron Burr trial for treason.

Lyceum Building, erected 1848, is center of University of Mississippi at Oxford.

Mississippi

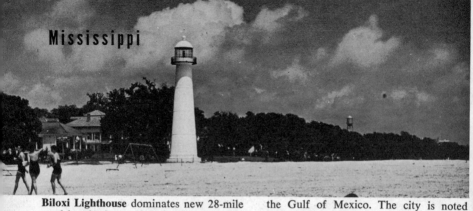

Biloxi Lighthouse dominates new 28-mile sand beach along Mississippi Sound, near the Gulf of Mexico. The city is noted as packing center for oysters and shrimp.

Swimming pool is one of Biloxi's many attractions for entertainment of tourists.

Percy Quinn State Park, at McComb, is one of eight state parks in Mississippi.

The Walter Place, Holly Springs, is fine example of a luxurious home of the 1850's.

Old Capitol Building, Jackson: Henry Clay, Jefferson Davis spoke from balcony

166

Photos: Mississippi Agricultural & Industrial Boar

LOUISIANA MEANS PLANTATIONS, BAYOUS, AND FABULOUS NEW ORLEANS

From balcony of Pontalba Apartments, visitors to New Orleans' historic *Vieux Carré* see famous St. Louis Cathedral, on Chartres Street and Jackson Square.

"Dinner at Antoine's" added fame to an already internationally known restaurant.

Above is exterior, and at left the front desk of Antoine Alciatore's restaurant.

French Market coffee stand is place for coffee and doughnuts in the wee hours.

Pirates Alley runs between St. Louis Cathedral and Cabildo, where Spanish ruled.

Old Absinthe House has secret room where Jackson met Laffite to plan city's defense

Photos: Antoine's Restaurant; Louisiana Department of Commerce and Industry; bottom right, Delta-C&S Air Lines

Browsing in the numerous antique shops is favorite occupation in the old French Quarter. Many buildings are adorned with lovely wrought-iron projecting balconies.

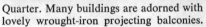

There are many shops, too, featuring the mouth-watering Creole pecan pralines.

Seen through intriguing doorways are magnificent patios, verdant courtyards.

Photos: Henri Cartier-Bresson (Magnum); Delta-C&S Air Lines

Tulane University's 93-acre campus is scene of the Sugar Bowl football game.

The International Trade Mart exhibits products from South America, Europe.

Huey P. Long Bridge is $13 million span carrying automobiles and trains across the Mississippi, which is 2,200 feet wide here, and as much as 180 feet deep.

Canal Street extends 3½ miles, from the Mississippi to Metairie. It is one of the widest thoroughfares in the world 171 feet, and one of most brilliantly l

Photos: Louisiana Department of Commerce a Industry; center, Bureau of New Orleans Ne

At Mardi Gras time, and on New Year's Eve, Canal Street is real maelstrom.

Mardi Gras, the festival that ushers in Lent, brings 100,000 visitors to the city.

The Mississippi winds around New Orleans in a great crescent, lined with docks for ships that have come down the river and ships that have come through the Gulf.

171

Louisiana

Memorial Tower clock and chimes keep time for students at Louisiana State.

Louisiana's towering Capitol at Baton Rouge soars 33 stories, cost $5 million.

Statue of Evangeline is in St. Martinville, the heart of the Acadian country.

Snowy egrets sun themselves in famous Bird City sanctuary at Avery Island.

Photos: Louisiana Department of Commerce and Industry

Still waters of Bayou Teche are guarded by cypress trees overhung with Spanish moss. Bridge in background crosses over into Longfellow-Evangeline State Park.

At Oakley, John James Audubon did much research for his great *Birds of America.*

San Francisco is "Steamboat Gothic" home, Garyville, built before Civil War.

One of loveliest of plantation homes is Greenwood, 1830–35, St. Francisville.

The Shadows, at New Iberia, stands in lush gardens bordering Bayou Teche.

But for the automboile on deck, this photo of the Mississippi at Baton Rouge might have been taken in Mark Twain's time. Ferries cross from Port Allen to city.

Pirogue races are held at Barataria Bay each year. Smugglers and pirates once made this their headquarters. It is now the heart of Louisiana's shrimp country

ARKANSAS IS HOME OF HOT SPRINGS, WORLD FAMOUS SPA

Along the lower reaches of the White River before it joins the Mississippi: Commercial fishing on Arkansas rivers brings an income of $1½ million annually.

Arkansas

Giant bluffs dwarf fishermen on a float trip down the White River. The Arkansas River, flowing nearly 1,500 miles from Rockies, is state's principal waterway.

Mystic Cave, above, Wonderland Cavern, Diamond Cave are underground marvels.

Eden Falls, Lost Valley: In mountain country, streams are clear, swift, cold.

Photos: Arkansas Publicity and Parks Commission, top by Harold Phelps

Hot Springs National Park, America's oldest, was dedicated in 1832. It covers 1,000 acres in Ouachita Mountains. View shows Army and Navy General Hospital.

Arkansas' old State House, in Little Rock, is now official history museum.

Beautiful new State Capitol, designed by Cass Gilbert, was finished in 1916.

Oaklawn Jockey Club, Hot Springs, has glass-enclosed, steam-heated grandstand. The climax of each meet is the Arkansas Derby, famous event for three-year-olds.

Little Rock Country Club is high above Arkansas River, once busy steamboat route. North Little Rock, on the other side of the river, is reached by five bridges

Railway ferry "Pelican" carries freight cars across the Mississippi at Helena.

Outboard motor racing is popular at Lake Hamilton, Hot Springs, and at Batesville

Arkansas Post State Park adjoins town which was first capital of the Territory.

Artistry of "land of cross-bow" is shown at Blanchard Springs, Mountain View

Photos: Arkansas Publicity and Parks Commission, bottom right by Harold Phelps; top, Little Rock Chamber of Commerce

TENNESSEE IS KNOWN FOR SMOKIES, T.V.A., ANDREW JACKSON, ATOM BOMB

Gatlinburg is on the edge of Great Smoky Mountains National Park, which covers 643 square miles in Tennessee and North Carolina. Photo shows the smoky mist.

Photo: Paul A. Moore,
Tenn. Conservation Dept.

"Gordon C. Greene" on the Tennessee River near Chattanooga: After the Civil War, more than fifty steamboats were in operation carrying passengers, freight.

Hiking party tackles Mt. LeConte, 6,595-foot peak in the Great Smoky Mountains.

Lookout Mountain Incline Railway goes from Chattanooga to summit of mountain.

Photos: Paul A. Moore,
Tenn. Conservation Dept.

Memphis, largest city in Tennessee, is a metropolis for that state and for the nearby states of Mississippi, Arkansas. It is named after ancient city on Nile.

Marble quarrying ranks with textiles and furniture as top Knoxville industries.

Spinning, hand-weaving, coverlet-making are prized arts of Tennessee mountain folk.

From top of Lookout Mountain, Chattanooga, you can see more than 100 miles on clear days. This vantage point is near upper end of Incline Railway (photo left).

Photos: Paul A. Moore, Tenn. Conservation Department; top, Delta-C&S Air Lines

Tennessee

Oak Ridge is site of laboratory at which uranium for the world's first two atom bombs was separated. Community housing 30,000 was built here almost "overnight."

Fort Negley, built 1862, overlooks Nashville from the summit of St. Cloud Hill.

Tennessee State Capitol stands on Cedar Knob, highest point in city of Nashville.

Reelfoot Lake, formed by earthquake in 1811, is noted for its huge cypress trees and abundant plant life. 18 miles long, 2½ miles wide, it's only 2 to 9 feet deep.

Photos: Paul A. Moore, Tenn. Conservation Dept.; center left, W. Lincoln Highton

Annual Cotton Carnival, in Memphis, tells story of city in pageantry. King Cotton and his Queen of Beauty reign for four days of revelry, parades, carnival balls.

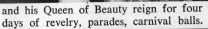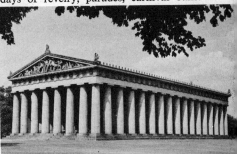

Parthenon, in Nashville's Centennial Park, is exact replica of the original in Athens.

Cotton Exchange, founded 1873, is the heart of Memphis and the cotton country.

Sewanee is the home of the University of the South, popularly known as "Sewanee."

Photos: Paul A. Moore,
Tenn. Conservation Dept.

The Hermitage, near Nashville, was home of Andrew Jackson, called "Old Hickory."

Vanderbilt University, at Nashville, is named for financier Cornelius Vanderbilt.

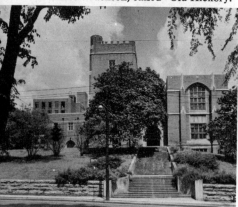

University of Tennessee occupies 40-acre campus crowning "The Hill" in Knoxville.

Home of James K. Polk, Columbia: The eleventh President practised law here.

Fall Creek Falls is slender column of water that dashes more than 250 feet.

Meriwether Lewis Monument honors co-leader of Lewis and Clark expedition.

Photos: Paul A. Moore, Tenn. Conservation Dept.

THE MIDWEST

Photo: Memorial Plaza, St. Louis,
by Massie—Missouri Resources Div.

185

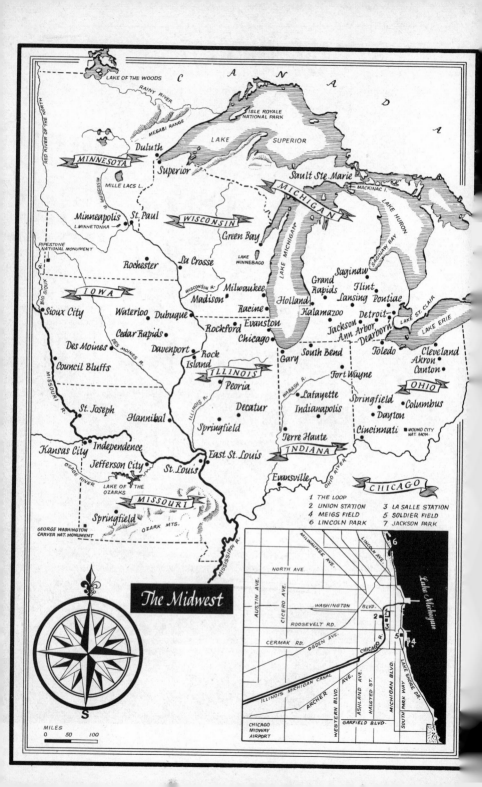

The Midwest

MILES
0   50   100

A 31-MILLION ACRE FARMLAND, ILLINOIS ALSO HAS GREAT MIDWEST METROPOLIS

Chicago, with more than 3½ million population, is the youngest of the world's great cities. Its nickname is the "Windy City." This is North Michigan Avenue.

Chicago River winds through the city, from Lake Michigan at left. Tremendous building at lower left is the Merchandis Mart, with 4 million feet of floor spac

eart of the business section is known The Loop, taking its name from the pattern made by elevated railway system. Chicago is 2nd largest city in the U.S.

Grant Park's 303 acres provide the mile-long Loop with an open view of the lake.

This is Buckingham Fountain, with the new Prudential skyscraper at the right.

Randolph Street is fun center of Loop at night, with theaters and night clubs.

Wrigley Building is across Michigan Avenue from Tribune Tower, Sheraton Hotel.

Flaming sword service is a distinctive feature of Pump Room, Ambassador East.

Photos: Kaufmann & Fabry Company; bottom left, Delta C&S Air Lines; bottom right, Shiro, Hotels Ambassador.

Oak Street Beach, most widely used public bathing spot, fills a corner on North Lake Shore Drive. Pedestrian tunnel connects it with Michigan Avenue and Drake Hotel.

Chicago's Union Stockyards are world's biggest; recently celebrated arrival of one-billionth animal. Nearby Amphitheater had the 1952 presidential conventions.

Merchandise Mart is second in floor area only to Pentagon Building, Washington.

Chicago Art Institute has 6,000 students, world-famous paintings and many exhibits.

Northwestern University has Chicago campus, above, for professional schools and divisions of night study. Main school i at Evanston, on shore of Lake Michigan

Rockefeller Memorial Chapel is one of stately University of Chicago buildings.

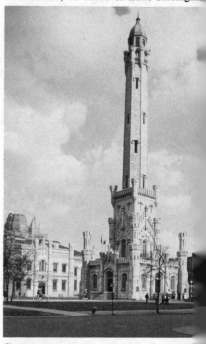

Chicago's great fire of 1871 spared t historic water tower, now much revere

Photos: Northwestern University; Wayne Mil University of Chicago; Kaufmann & Fabry Comp

Rodgers-Hammerstein Night brought big crowd to the Band Shell in Grant Park.

Nationally known guest conductors and soloists are featured at free concerts.

Garfield Park Conservatory has 5,000 species of flowers, valued at $1½ million.

Air view shows North Lake Shore Drive sweeping southward from Lincoln Park.

Lincoln Tomb, in Oak Ridge Cemetery, Springfield, was financed by citizens all over the nation. 117-ft. monument has four bronze groups and statue of Lincoln

Lincoln Log Cabin State Park has cabin lived in by Lincoln's father, stepmother.

This is Lincoln-Berry store, now in Ne Salem State Park, northwest of Springfiel

Photos: Illinois Divisi
of Department Repo

Cave-in-Rock, now State Park, was once the lair of Ohio River pirates, outlaws.

Time rolls back millions of years for those who explore canyons of Giant City Park.

Dyche Stadium, Northwestern University, at Evanston, can accommodate 54,000 at football games. McGaw Hall, background, is used for indoor meets, convocations.

Illinois

Since 1850, Illinois has been a top-rank agricultural state, and today its 195,000

farms are valued at $5 billion. 43 fi crops are grown, with corn the large

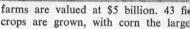

General U. S. Grant received this Galena home as gift on his return from Civil War.

This house in Springfield is the or home that Abraham Lincoln ever owne

"Wedding of the Wine and Cheese" is a feature of the annual grape festival at

Nauvoo, historic old Mormon city bui by the Mormon prophet, Joseph Smit

Photos: Illinois Division of Departme Reports; bottom, Illinois Division of Par

INDIANA, THE HOOSIER STATE, ADDS
BUSTLING INDUSTRY TO RURAL CHARM

acred **Heart Church** and Administration   of Notre Dame University at South Bend,
uilding with Golden Dome are features   home of Rockne's "Four Horsemen."

oto: University of Notre Dame   **197**

Executive Building houses administrative offices of Purdue University, noted for engineering courses. Behind it is Hall of Music Auditorium, seating 6,200 people.

Student Building is outstanding landmark of Indiana University, at Bloomington.

The French Lick Springs Hotel has bee known since 1840 as a luxurious resor

198

Indianapolis Motor Speedway, built 1909, is site of the annual 500-mile automobile speed classic. Some 150,000 attend the race, held each year on Memorial Day.

Trotting races are feature of Indiana State Fair, held each September at the Indianapolis Fairgrounds. It's been an annual feature for over a hundred years.

Indiana

Soldiers' and Sailors' Monument marks heart of Indianapolis, state's chief city.

At far end of impressive World War I Memorial Plaza is the Central Library.

Indiana State House is located on 9-acre square in downtown Indianapolis. Erected in 1878–88, of Indiana limestone, it Neo-Roman design. Basement is Museum

Photos: Indianapo
Chamber of Commer

Lincoln Memorial, Lincoln State Park: It was in this neighborhood that Lincoln's family settled in 1816, when he was 7, and Indiana had just been made a state.

From all over world, Christmas parcels come to be mailed from Santa Claus, Ind.

Oldest covered bridge in state, once at Raccoon, now spans Clinton Falls creek.

City park in New Harmony has "golden rain trees" brought from China by Wm. Maclure. These small round-topped trees produce large yellow flowers in June.

Indiana

Lanier mansion, at Madison, was thought "last word" when built, 100 years ago.

Indiana Dunes State Park covers 3½ sq. miles on southern tip of Lake Michigan.

Wyandotte Cave is one of largest in the country, with its 23 miles of passages.

Brown County State Park and adjoining Game Preserve constitute largest publicly

owned land in Indiana. Ten miles of fir roads show off this lovely hill countr

Photos: Indiana Department Commerce and Public Relatic

OHIO FARMS AND INDUSTRIES ARE SERVED BY LAKE ERIE, OHIO RIVER

Cleveland, Ohio's largest city, is big center for steel mills and refineries.

Ohio farm and range lands cover 22 million acres, with corn the major field crop.

Ohio

Cleveland from Lake Erie: At left is the Municipal Stadium. The city's landmark, tower of Union Terminal, dominates the background. City population is 914,808.

Ohio's Capitol, at Columbus, is one of purest examples of Greek Doric in U.S.

Toledo is 3rd largest railroad center of nation, with new Central Union Terminal.

Zanesville is divided into three parts by the Licking and Muskingum rivers. It is noted as site of only "Y" Bridg in country, spanning both of the river:

204

Akron is known as rubber capital of the world. B. F. Goodrich Rubber Company, above, produces automobile tires and over 30,000 kinds of other rubber articles.

Akron is the chief supplier of tires to nearby automobile-making city of Detroit.

Molten steel is "teemed" into molds at Republic Steel's plant at Cleveland.

Ohio

New group of "fledglings" is graduated from Ohio University, oldest college in what was formerly Northwest Territory. Ohio now has 52 colleges and universities.

Memorial at Ft. Recovery marks site of General Wayne's defeat of Indians, 1794.

Air view of Ohio State University, Columbus, shows 400-acre campus, stadium

206

Memorial at Hamilton reproduces stockade used in campaigns against the Indians.

Wright Brothers Monument, Dayton, honors inventors of first successful plane.

Allen Memorial Art Building at Oberlin was modeled after Brunelleschi's Hospital of the Innocents. It houses the finest college art museum in the United States.

Campus Martius Museum, at Marietta, has wonderful collection of pioneer relics,

including restoration of Rufus Putnam house, built by one of the first settlers.

Photos: Ohio Development and Publicity Commission, bottom left by S. Durward Hoag; center, Arthur E. Princehorn

Ohio

Ohio Caverns, West Liberty, are noted for coloring and diversity of formations.

Old Man's Cave, at Logan, is overhanging ledge that once formed home for hermit.

Constructed of stone and yellow clay by prehistoric Indians, the Great Serpent Mount extends for 1,330 feet. It is the most remarkable effigy mound in the U. S

Photos: Ohio Developmen and Publicity Commissic

River Rouge Plant of the Ford Motor Company, near Dearborn, is one of largest mass-production automobile factories in world. Henry Ford was born at Dearborn.

Michigan

Detroit, nation's fifth city, is noted as automobile-manufacturing center, with plants of General Motors, Chrysler, and others. It fronts on the Detroit River

A new Chevrolet, just completed, gets polish before assembly line inspection.

New Chryslers near the finish of the intricate step-by-step assembly process

Willow Run is one of world's largest manufacturing plants, built to produce bombers during World War II, and now used by General Motors for transmissions

210

Photos: Michigan Tourist Council; General Motors Corporation; Chrysler Corporation

Isle Royale National Park, rock fortress in Lake Superior, is a real wilderness.

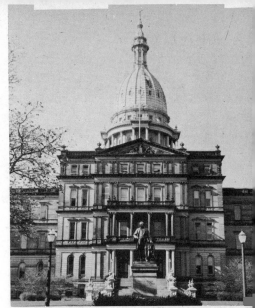

Lansing's skyline is dominated by the State Capitol and 25-story Olds Tower.

Greenfield Village, at Dearborn, was established by Henry Ford in 1933 to

re-create a colonial village. At left is Martha-Mary Chapel, above, old mill.

General Store at Greenfield Village complete with Cigar Store Indian.

Village also has river boat, and complete reproduction of Edison's first laboratory.

Photos: National Park Service; Michigan Tourist Council; center right and bottom, Dr. Jacob E. Klein

211

Michigan

The "Soo" Locks at Sault Ste. Marie enable the lake boats to travel along the canal between Lake Huron and Lake Superior, avoiding St. Mary's rapids.

Carriages line main street of autoless resort on historic Mackinac Island.

Porch of Mackinac's luxurious Grand Hotel is said to be world's longest.

Straits of Mackinac cut Michigan in two, between the Upper Peninsula and the Lower Peninsula. Ferries take autos and their passengers across this barrier.

Photos: Michigan Tourist Council

University of Michigan is at Ann Arbor, on Huron River. This is Law Quadrangle.

Tahquamenon Falls: This river plays prominent part in Longfellow's Hiawatha.

On opening day of Tulip Festival in city of Holland, citizens don their Dutch cos-tumes and literally scrub the streets. Merchants scrub sidewalks by their stores.

Port Huron, on St. Clair River, connects with Canada by an international bridge.

Lake o' the Clouds is high in the Upper Peninsula's remote Porcupine Mountains.

Photos: Michigan Tourist Council; Center, Holland Chamber of Commerce

213

Michigan

Ishpeming is the ski center of Northern Michigan, with one of state's first clubs.

State has 18 million acres of farm a range land, varied field and truck cro

Interlochen is scene of summer music camps for high school boys and girls.

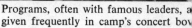

Programs, often with famous leaders, a given frequently in camp's concert bo

Pictured Rocks, multicolored cliffs on Lake Superior shore, extend 27 miles.

Memorial on Au Sable River perpetua spirit of Michigan's pioneer lumberm

214

LAKES, WATERFALLS, GREEN WOODS
BLESS WISCONSIN'S VACATIONLAND

Wisconsin has some 8,500 lakes, 10,000 miles of trout streams, and 500 miles of shoreline on Lakes Superior, Michigan. This is High Lake, near Michigan border.

Photo: Wisconsin Con-
servation Department

215

Wisconsin

From dome of State Capitol, Madison, you can see five lakes. Three girdle city,

Lakes Mendota, Monona and Wing Lakes Kegonsa and Waubesa are near

Wisconsin River is one of many stream in Badger State for canoeing, fishin

Near Wisconsin Dells, seven miles of sandstone rocks have been etched by river.

First Capitol Building, at Old Belmon was used by the legislature in 183

Photos: Wisconsin Co servation Departme

At Pattison State Park, the Black River plunges 165 feet over Big Manitou Falls.

U. S. Forest Products Laboratory, Madison, conducts research on the use of wood.

A summertime class at the University of Wisconsin meets below Carillon Tower.

t. Croix River cuts through castellated luffs in Interstate Park, recreation area that is shared between Wisconsin and Minnesota. Park covers 730 acres.

Devils Lake is hemmed in by horseshoe of cliffs, some 500 feet high. Formed by glacial action, it is a paradise for geological students hunting its oddities.

Tank Cottage, at Green Bay, is the oldest house standing in Wisconsin, built 1776.

Villa Louis was built at Prairie du Chic by the fur-trader, Hercules L. Dousma

Potawatomi State Park, on the peninsula between Green Bay and Lake Michigan, is one of Wisconsin's 21 state par Many trails wind through Norway pin

218

THE "SHOW ME!" STATE OF MISSOURI IS CENTER OF TRANSPORTATION AND COMMERCE

...issouri River joins the Mississippi ...st above St. Louis. Including its 500- mile frontage on the Mississippi, state has over 1,000 miles of navigable water.

...to: Massie—Missouri Resources Div.

Missouri KANSAS CITY, ST. LOUIS

Union Station with downtown Kansas City skyline: On route of the Santa Fe and Oregon trails, Kansas City is today important railroad and airline cente

Kansas City's Eleventh Street area has the major stores, theaters and hotels.

Liberty Memorial is 217-foot shaft, honor of those serving in World War

Swope Park, with 1,346 acres of hill ravines is the 3rd largest U.S. city par

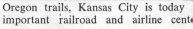

Photos: bottom left, G. A. Rein Massie—Missouri Resources D

Jefferson Memorial, St. Louis, is built on site of Louisiana Purchase Exposition.

Shaw's Garden, modeled after London's Kew Gardens, has 12,000 plant species.

t. Louis, state's largest city, is 2nd only Chicago in importance as railway cen- ter. Union Station, with train sheds and power house, covers more than 20 acres.

Missouri

Mark Twain statue, at Hannibal, looks out over river he immortalized in books.

"Tom Sawyer" and "Huckleberry Finn" of today watch stern-wheeler on Mississippi

"Tom and Huck" statue is said to be first one to commemorate characters of fiction.

Tom Sawyer's fence: He persuaded gang to pay for privilege of whitewashing

222

Lake of the Ozarks, 129 miles long, is one of the largest wholly artificial lakes in country. Innumerable wooded coves make for good boating, fishing and swimming.

Stern-wheeler "Avalon" represents the old as she ties up at Cape Girardeau dock.

Modern excursion steamer "Admiral" conveys today's tourists along the river.

eramec Cavern has room with parking ace for 300 autos. This is the "Stage."

These columns are all that remain of first hall of University of Missouri, Columbia.

otos: Massie—Missouri Resources Div.

Missouri

Thomas Hart Benton's lively murals are in house lounge of Capitol, Jefferson City.

Missouri's capital, known locally as "Jeff City" is named after Thomas Jefferson.

Home of Ex-President Truman is in town of Independence, in western Missouri.

Santa-Cali-Gon Parade, at Independence commemorates days of wagon caravans

Champion mules: Missouri mules have long been known for quality, mulishness!

Henry County is noted for its dairy an poultry farms, for these Roberts' horse

Photos: Massie—Missouri Resources D

IOWA, SYMBOL OF CORN BELT IS RICHEST FARM STATE

d **Capitol Building,** Iowa City, now ministrative center of State University

of Iowa, was State Capitol from 1846 to 1857, when Des Moines became capital.

oto: State University of Iowa

Old water mill, Panora: Town's name is contraction of "panorama," the story be- ing that pioneers, viewing site from a hi exclaimed, "What a beautiful panorama

Davenport stretches along Mississippi River for five miles, where it widens to form Lake Davenport. Rock Isla and Moline, Illinois, are across rive

226

Photo: Iowa Development Commiss'

State Capitol looks down on Des Moines River from an eminence east of the Des Moines. Design of the gilded dome recalls that of the Hotel des Invalides in Paris.

About 30% of Iowa's land is in pasture, with the eastern and western sections leading in meat production, the northwestern part being chief dairying region.

227

Iowa is symbol of the Corn Belt, with 95% of the land in farms. The state leads the nation in corn and oats, in ho poultry and eggs, and in fattening ca

Cutler Bridge, Madison County: Most of the state is a gently rolling plain, with many winding rivers. Hilly northeast region is called "Little Switzerlan

228

Photos: Iowa Development Com sion, top left by James A. K

0,000 LAKES, BEAUTIFUL FORESTS
LURE VISITORS TO MINNESOTA

it Rock Lighthouse, on sheer cliff high
ve Lake Superior, warns of dangerous
reefs. Light and siren are important because metal in rocks throws compasses off.

to: W. A. Fisher, courtesy Lake
erior North Shore Association

Minnesota

At Silver Creek Cliff, the highway from Duluth to Canada follows the scenic north shore of Lake Superior. Nearby is l made famous in *Hiawatha,* Gitche Gum

Winter waves of Lake Superior pile up windrows of ice, 20 feet high, miles long.

John Jacob Astor trading post was cen of fur trading more than 100 years a

Mighty Mississippi, "Father of Water has its source here, in Itasca State Par

Ice-bound Iron Ore Carriers: Frequently ships trying to open the season early find further headway impossible. Th they must wait for a shift in the wir

Photos: Barney Thomas; top, W. A. Fisher; low center right, Minnesota Division of Publi

Minneapolis is state's largest city, the banking and wholesale center of the area.

It adjoins St. Paul, Minnesota's capital, and the two are known as "Twin Cities."

ur trappers use skis to run their lines the wilderness of Northern Minnesota.

Palisade Head is 80-acre headland of volcanic rock jutting from Lake Superior.

Air view of St. Paul shows Capitol at upper left, main business section with

First National Bank skyscraper, and three of many bridges across Mississippi

Girl scouts paddle huge "war canoe" near their camp on Northern Minnesota lake.

Giant statues of Paul Bunyan and his Blue Ox stand on shore of Lake Bemidji

Falls of Minnehaha, immortalized in poem by Longfellow, are in Minneapolis park.

Kensington Runestone, shown in replica, says Vikings came to Minnesota in 1362

232

Photos: Kenneth M. Wright; center left, Barr Thomas; center right, Minnesota Division Publicity; bottom left, Northwest Orient Airlines

THE PLAINS STATES

Photo: From summit of Scotts Bluff National
Monument, by Division of Nebraska Resources

233

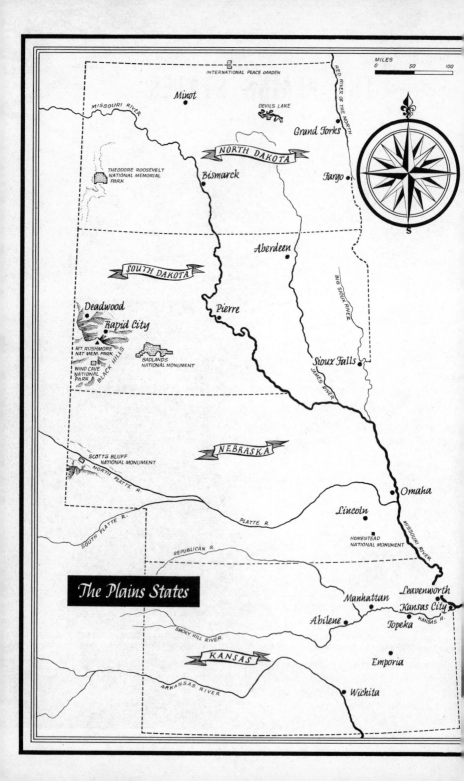

NORTH DAKOTA HAS UNBOUNDED PLAINS, HILLS, COLORFUL BADLANDS

Riders explore Theodore Roosevelt National Memorial Park, in Badlands of the Little Missouri. Park honors the President who ranched here as a youth, 1883–86.

North Dakota

Logging camp near Little Missouri River was used to cut ties for building of the Northern Pacific Railway. Bunkhouse had rifle loopholes to ward off Indian raids.

Combines in North Dakota wheat field: State leads all others in production of rye and durum wheat, is second in barley. Most of state is crop and pasture land.

Photos: Greater North Dakota Association; Northwest Orient Airlines

This marker notes geographical center of North America, at Rugby, North Dakota.

Monument on Missouri River at Sanish honors the French explorer, La Verendrye.

North Dakota's 19-story State Capitol overlooks Bismarck and Missouri valley.

Oil well rig towers above flat prairie of Beaver Lodge Field, south of Tioga.

17 inches of water spill over gates of Baldhill Dam and its irrigation reservoir.

Fort McKeen blockhouse stands in Fort Abraham Lincoln State Park, at Mandan.

North Dakota

These columnar cedars, known as "upside-down trees," are the only known growth of this species in the world. Nearby is North Dakota's famous Burning Coal Mine.

This cairn marks boundary between Canada, U.S. in International Peace Garden.

Lake adds loveliness to Peace Garden, shared by Manitoba and North Dakota.

Photos: Greater North Dakota Association

SOUTH DAKOTA IS SCENE OF FAMOUS
BLACK HILLS AND MOUNT RUSHMORE

The Dakota Indians named this colorful and deeply eroded country *makosica*, or "bad land." Now a National Monument, the Badlands is labyrinth of odd shapes.

Photo: Alfred E. Reichenberger

South Dakota

The Badlands has 640,000 acres of jagged peaks, deep canyons. Once an ocean bed, then a swamp and now a desert, this area contains many land and marine fossils.

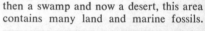

Harney Peak, 7,242 feet, is highest in the Black Hills and highest in state.

Sylvan Lake, called by Indians "Tear in Mountains," is 6,300 feet above sea level.

240

Photos: Publicity Department, South Dakota State Highway Commission

The herd of buffalo at pasture in Custer State Park numbers close to a thousand.

Calvin Coolidge used Game Lodge in the park as his Summer White House in 1927.

Mount Rushmore National Memorial has giant heads of Washington, Jefferson,

Theodore Roosevelt, Lincoln, sculptured by Gutzon Borglum and his son, Lincoln.

South Dakota

Highway through Custer Park takes you past these impressive "Cathedral Spires."

South Dakota State Capitol is at Pierre, where the Bad and Missouri rivers join

Soldiers' & Sailors' World War Memorial is another point of interest in Pierre.

Homestake, in town of Lead, is larges gold mine in U.S., discovered in 1876

Wind Cave has formations quite unlike those in any other National Park cave.

Dinosaur Park is museum of prehistor creatures at the state School of Mine

Photos: Publicity Department, Sou
Dakota State Highway Commissi

"CORNHUSKER STATE" OF NEBRASKA MERGES MIDDLE WEST WITH WEST

braska is one of the country's highest-.king states in growing wheat, corn, rye, hay. The sand hills areas raise much livestock. Most of land is farmed.

Nebraska

Mitchell Pass, near Scottsbluff, is one of the landmarks of the old Oregon Trail.

Ruts worn by covered wagons of the pioneers moving westward can still be se

Nebraska's State House, Lincoln, towers 400 feet, is topped by symbolic "Sower."

Graduates of the University of Nebras parade on the orderly campus at Linco

244

Beef cattle judging at Nebraska State Fair: The huge 287-acre Fairgrounds at Lincoln attract thousands of visitors to Fair held each September since 1900.

Union Stockyards, Omaha: Largest city state, Omaha is a leading meat-packing and stockyard center, and it leads all the world's cities in butter production.

Kingsley Dam forms Lake McConaughy, with storage capacity of two million acre-feet of water for irrigation. It is one of largest earth-filled dams in U.S.

Nebraska

The Burlington "Hump" on the western outskirts of Lincoln is considered one of nation's finest freight assembly yards It is a marvel of modern traffic contro

J. Sterling Morton, who instituted Arbor Day, lived in this Nebraska City mansion.

Joslyn Memorial Art Museum, Omah has Early Renaissance, other exhibit

Soldier Creek winds through the 36,000-acre Fort Robinson Military Reservation.

Homestead National Monument is site first land claimed under Homestead L

246

Photos: Division
Nebraska Resou

KANSAS, GRASS PRAIRIE AND HIGH PLAINS, IS GEOGRAPHICAL CENTER OF U.S.A.

...nsas produces most hard winter wheat, ...out 20% of nation's supply. 48 million acres are in farm and range land. State slopes from 4,000 feet in west to 750.

Kansas

Monument Rocks, sometimes known as "the Kansas pyramids," rise abruptly from the High Plains, in valley of Smoky Hil River. At north end is "Kansas sphinx."

This house at Abilene was the boyhood home of President Dwight D. Eisenhower.

At right is Eisenhower Memorial which houses President's souvenirs, mementos

William Allen White made little *Emporia Gazette* a nationally respected newspaper.

State Capitol at Topeka contains striki John Brown mural by John Steuart Cur

248

Kansas State College, originally Bluemont College, has its campus at Manhattan.

Design of the Kansas Capitol is based on that of the Capitol at Washington.

Scott County Lake is typical of meager natural bodies of water in the state.

World's largest municipal free swimming pool, 337 x 218 feet, is at Garden City.

Patton Hall, Fort Riley: This is only avalry school maintained by U. S. Army.

Salt mining, Lyons: Minerals are second in importance to agriculture in Kansas.

Kansas

Three Kansas landmarks: Campanile at the University of Kansas, in Lawrence. Cowboy statue in Boothill Park, Dod City. Madonna of Trail, Council Grov

Wyandotte County Lake and Park are in outskirts of industrial Kansas City.

Indian burial pit is point of intere near the flour-milling city of Salin

Dodge City is keen for sporting events, motorcycle races, dog and horse races.

At right is cairn near Lebanon markin geographic center of the United States

250

THE ROCKY MOUNTAINS

noto: Little Chief Mountain and St. Mary Lake,
lacier National Park, Montana, by Grant M. Haist

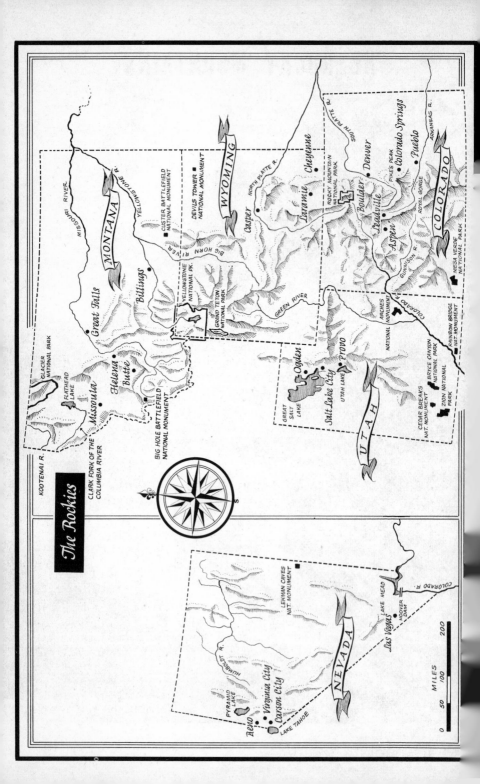

The Rockies

MONTANA

WYOMING

COLORADO

UTAH

NEVADA

KOOTENAI R.

CLARK FORK OF THE COLUMBIA RIVER

GLACIER NATIONAL PARK

FLATHEAD LAKE

Missoula

MISSOURI RIVER

Great Falls

Helena

Butte

YELLOWSTONE R.

Billings

BIG HOLE BATTLEFIELD NATIONAL MONUMENT

CUSTER BATTLEFIELD NATIONAL MONUMENT

DEVILS TOWER NATIONAL MONUMENT

BIG HORN RIVER

YELLOWSTONE NATIONAL PK.

GRAND TETON NATIONAL PARK

GREEN RIVER

Casper

NORTH PLATTE R.

SOUTH PLATTE R.

Laramie

Cheyenne

ROCKY MOUNTAIN NATIONAL PARK

Boulder

Denver

Colorado Springs

PIKES PEAK

Leadville

Aspen

Pueblo

ARKANSAS R.

GUNNISON R.

ROYAL GORGE

COLORADO R.

MESA VERDE NATIONAL PARK

RAINBOW BRIDGE NAT. MONUMENT

ARCHES NATIONAL

Ogden

Provo

UTAH LAKE

Salt Lake City

GREAT SALT LAKE

BRYCE CANYON NATIONAL PARK

CEDAR BREAKS NAT. MONUMENT

ZION NATIONAL PARK

LEHMAN CAVES NAT. MONUMENT

HUMBOLDT R.

PYRAMID LAKE

Reno

Virginia City

Carson City

LAKE TAHOE

LAKE MEAD

HOOVER DAM

Las Vegas

COLORADO R.

MILES

0   50   100   200

N S

GLACIER NATIONAL PARK IS ONE OF MONTANA'S MANY WONDERS

Glacier National Park is magnificent glacier-carved region astride Continental Divide. Two Medicine Lake is one of 200 lakes, set against the spectacular peaks.

Photo: Great Northern Railway

St. Mary Lake's dark blue waters mirror great peaks, some over 9,500 feet high.

Lake McDonald, largest lake in Glaci— National Park, is 10 miles long and ov—

Glacier Park Hotel adjoins the Great Northern Railway station at easterly entrance to the park. There are fo— hotels and three chalets for visito—

a mile wide. Because of its depth, up to 437 feet, it is frequently ice-free all winter, though the banks may be deep with snow. Fly-fishing is good here.

Trails in Glacier National Park total some 900 miles, and trail tours are very popular. Others prefer hiking, climbing, auto tours, fishing, or just plain looking.

Photos: Top, Glacier National Park, by ...leman; bottom, Great Northern Railway

Montana

Montana's Capitol, at Helena, is viewed from "Last Chancer," popular tour train named after Last Chance Gulch where discovery of gold was made in 1864

Algeria Shrine Temple and nearby Hill Park are two points of interest in Helena.

St. Helena Roman Catholic Cathedral modeled after one at Cologne, Germany

256

Lewis and Clark National Forest, named for the leaders of the epic expedition, is one of 11 national forests in Montana. Four trail riders follow the Chinese Wall.

Prospectors still pan for gold, convinced that sooner or later they'll strike it rich.

Midland Empire Fair, at Billings, features rodeo in which ranking riders compete.

Hungry Horse Dam forms a 30-mile-long reservoir south of Glacier National Park.

Visitors to Lewis and Clark Cavern are awed by the 26-foot Empire State Column.

Photos: Montana Highway Commission; top, U. S. Forest Service; center right, bottom left, Northwest Orient Airlines.

Montana

Winter scene near Billings: Montana has every advantage for winter sports— plenty of snow and clear, cold weather; hilly country; people with skiing traditions.

Sheep grazing: Montana ranks high in production of wool from flocks like this.

Cowboys separate calves from cows. Chi livestock markets are Miles City, Billing

258

tte, second largest city in state, is own as "richest hill on earth," pro- ducing almost a third of copper mined in the U.S., zinc, silver and manganese.

are albino buffalo is one of herd of **0** bison on the National Bison Range.

University Hall is center of campus at Montana State University, at Missoula.

ster Battlefield National Monument **rks** "Last Stand" made by Col. George Armstrong Custer and his 263 soldiers before massacre by Sioux and Cheyennes.

Montana

Cowboy gets light from red-hot branding iron, on one of state's many dude ranches.

Native blackspot trout and Dolly Varden abound in larger streams, northwest lakes

In Virginia City, rejuvenated gold camp town, actors re-enact stage-coach robbery.

Indian pow-wow on Flathead Reservation features performance of old ceremonies

Dark soils of north and east prairies make state a major producer of wheat.

John Lewis Clark, Indian sculptor, carves miniature wild animals of native wood

Photos: top, Northwest Orient Airlines; cent Montana Highway Commission, E. N. Harrison; botto Ray J. Manley, Charles W. Herbert (Western Way

YELLOWSTONE PARK HEADS WYOMING'S LIST OF NATURE'S MARVELS

llowstone National Park is largest and **lest** of our national parks, established 1872. Best-known geyser is Old Faithful which spouts 140 feet every 65 minutes.

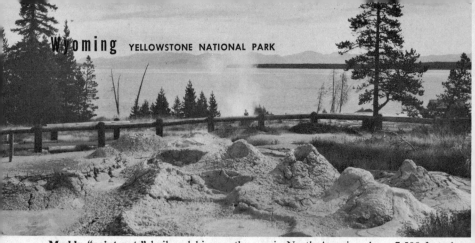

Muddy "paint pots" boil and hiss on the shore of Yellowstone Lake, largest lake in North America above 7,500 feet elevation. It spreads over 138 square miles.

Upper Falls of the Yellowstone may be seen from two platforms, one at the head and one halfway down the side of th 112-foot cataract in its 50-foot channe

Photos: Bill Sears (Western Way bottom, Northern Pacific Railw

reat columns of steam rise from 18 or ore geysers in Norris Geyser Basin, named after Philetus W. Norris, one of the early superintendents of the park.

ower Falls of the Yellowstone, plunging ver 300 feet, is park's most spectacular sight. Below the falls is Grand Canyon of the Yellowstone in 1,000-foot gorge.

The Church of the Transfiguration, built of logs, has only one room. It nestles against the Grand Teton Mountains, ne far from Jackson Hole and Jackson Lake

Picture window behind the altar in Church of the Transfiguration frames magnificent view of the sharp, ragged peaks of th Teton Range, 22 of them over 10,000 feet

Photos: Grant M. Hais
bottom, Willard Lu

Menor's Flatboat Ferry crosses Snake River at Moose, in shadow of the Grand Tetons. It started operation in 1892, and was authentically restored in 1949.

Jenny Lake reflects the blue-green woods and cathedral spires of Teton Mountains.

This twisted aspen tree is favorite of camera fans in Grand Teton National Park.

Wyoming

Below Jackson, the Snake River flows through forested hills, in its twisting, winding course. The channel is known as the Grand Canyon of the Snake River.

Rugged mountain scenery greets visitors along the Cody Road to Yellowstone Park.

Devils Tower was first National Monument, named by Theodore Roosevelt, 1906.

Photos: Willard Luce; Burlington Route; Wyoming Travel Commission

With 3½ million sheep and lambs, Wyoming ranks next to Texas in the production of mutton, wool. State's 33 million acres of farmland are mostly for sheep, cattle.

Speed demons of the West: This unusual camera shot of a group of fast-scurrying antelope was made from low-flying plane. They make long migrations, seeking food.

There are more than 30,000 elk in the state, divided into several herds. Over 10,000 are fed hay each winter in Teton Forest Game Sanctuary, Jackson Hole.

Wyoming

Black and brown bears enjoy Yellowstone Park almost as much as human visitors do.

Teton Mountains edging Jackson Lak[e] give it a setting of Alpine lovelines[s]

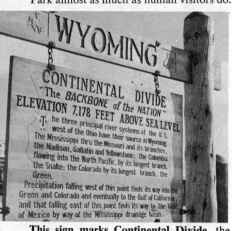

This sign marks Continental Divide, the 7,178-foot-high "backbone of the nation."

Climax of most Wyoming rodeos is "wild[ ]race, with horses never before ridder[n]

Mount Moran: Wyoming's great ranges include Bighorn Mountains, Absaroka

Range in the east, peaks of Yellowston[e] Park in northwest, and Tetons in west

268

COLORADO'S RUGGED BEAUTY BOASTS
51 PEAKS OVER 14,000 FEET HIGH

Colorado has highest average altitude of any state, 6,800 feet, with Continental Divide of the Rocky Mountains running across the state from north to south.

Colorado

Colorado National Monument is 18,000-acre wonderland. These are "coke ovens."

Rocky Mountain National Park has 40½ square miles of mountains and lakes

Mesa Verde National Park preserves the remarkable homes of the Cliff Dwellers.

Black Canyon of the Gunnison National Monument includes 10 miles of gorge.

Photos: D. L. Hopwood; Burlington Route; Willard Luce; Colorado Advertising & Publicity Department

Pikes Peak, 14,110 feet, may be climbed by car, or by cog railroad from Manitou Springs. Auto race to the top is held annually on winding Pikes Peak Highway.

Photo: Colorado Advertising & Publicity Department

Colorado

Statue of Broncho Buster in Denver's Civic Center typifies life of cowboys.

Red Rocks Amphitheater, Denver Mountain Parks, has a capacity of 10,00

View from Civic Center shows how near Denver, the "Mile High City," is to the Rockies. City and County Building, abov faces the State Capitol across the Cente

Balanced Rock is one of natural marvels in Garden of the Gods, Manitou Springs.

Mushroom Park is another of many weir rock formations in Garden of the God

272

Photos: D. L. Hopwood; top le
G. A. Reims; center, Burlington Rou

There are plenty of thrills and spills at Colorado rodeos throughout the summer.

In winter, skiing is favorite sport at Aspen, Winter Park, Berthoud Pass, etc.

Royal Gorge, or Grand Canyon of the Arkansas, has sheer 1,000-foot walls.

Royal Gorge Suspension Bridge, carrying highway across, is highest in the world.

Photos: Glenn U. Nichols; Chas. Grover; D. L. Hopwood

Colorado

About 7 million acres of the state's Great Plains area is devoted to wheat raising.

Some 800 descendants of Colorado's onc numerous Indians live on one reservation

Great Sand Dunes, named as a National Monument, 1932, cover 80 square miles.

The mounds, constantly changing, ofte rise to heights of more than 1,500 fee

Red Rock Lake, with Indian Peaks in the background, is in the Roosevelt National

Forest. State has 20 million acres c forest and many fine trails for hikin

274

Photos: D. L. Hopwood; top right, Alfred Reichenberger; bottom, U. S. Forest Servic

urkey ranch: Raising of poultry, cattle, ogs and horses is important activity.

Quarries yield granite, marble, limestone, sandstone, lava, other building stones.

inosaur National Monument has skeletal mains of dinosaurs, prehistoric reptiles.

Wheeler National Monument has striking varicolored configurations of sandstone.

Estes Park is mountain playground and resort on eastern side of Rocky Mountain

National Park. It is in lovely vall near Longs Peak, other lofty mountain

Grand Lake is extremely deep; in places the lake bottom has never been sounded.

Crater Lake mirrors Lone Eagle Pea State has 1,500 peaks over 10,000 fee

Photos: D. L. Hopwoo
top, Konstantin Kost

UTAH OUTRANKS ALL STATES
IN WONDERS OF NATURE

This natural bridge is one of best known landmarks of Bryce Canyon National Park. Over 70% of Utah's beautiful land is in U.S. ownership, as parks and forests.

oto: Willard Luce

Bryce Canyon National Park has 100,000 visitors a year to view amazing area

the Piaute Indians called "red rocks standing like men in a bowl shaped canyon

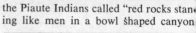

Bryce is entered at rim of the canyon, with trails leading down to the floor.

Almost every conceivable shape is found in Bryce, and some sixty different tints

Photos: National Park Service;
Grant M. Haist; Willard Lu

Zion National Park is noted for scenic grandeur. This is First Patriarch Peak.

Grand Arch Lookout views Mt. Carmel highway, climbing 800 feet in 3 miles.

The Great White Throne is best-known of the monoliths in Zion National Park.

Checkerboard Mesa shows unusual result of nature's action on porous sandstone.

Photos: Willard Luce

Landscape Arch, 292 feet, is considered longest natural span in the world. It is located in Devils Garden section Arches National Monument, near Moa

The Double Arch, sometimes called the "jughandles," is in The Windows section.

Delicate Arch, alone and sharp agains sky, is one of most popular with visitors

280

Photos: Willard Luce

Millet had been American, says Henri Cartier-Bresson, he would have painted this instead of the Angelus. Scene is at beginning of Rockies, beyond Salt Lake.

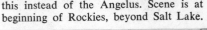

Hackberry Canyon Ruins show beautiful one work of Hovenweep Monument.

Point Supreme overlooks Cedar Breaks National Monument, surpassing Bryce.

Photos: Henri Cartier-Bresson (Magnum); bottom, Willard Luce

Sailing is one of principal recreational activities on Great Salt Lake, largest inland body of salt water in the Western Hemisphere, 75 miles long and 40 wide

Impressive monument marks spot where Brigham Young said, "This is the place."

State Capitol building, Salt Lake City, is seen from gardens of the Hotel Utah

Mormon Temple took 40 years to build, with granite hauled 28 miles by oxen.

City and County building, Salt Lake City, served as the capitol from 1894 to 1915

Photos: Willard Luce

Newly-completed Pioneer Memorial Museum is near Capitol, in Wasatch foothills.

Guide tells tourists, at Seagull Monument, how gulls saved starving pioneers.

The Lion House was home of Brigham Young, Mormon leader, and many wives.

This little cabin, preserved on Temple Square, was one of first built by settlers.

Photos: Willard Luce

Rainbow Bridge National Monument was established by President Taft in 1910.

It includes 160 acres around the great arch, 308 feet high and 275 feet across.

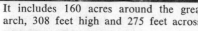

The Narrows is 18-foot cleft in Capitol Gorge, Capitol Reef National Monument.

Utah Copper Mine, near Bingham Canyon, is world's largest open pit copper mine.

Photos: Willard Luce; top Ray Manley (Western Ways)

Remnant of old movie set stands beneath impressive butte in Professor Valley a few miles up the Colorado River from Moab, in southeastern part of the state.

These mountain meadows are below timberline of 12,008-foot Mount Timpanogos.

Mile-long zigzag trail leads to entrance of Timpanogos Cave National Monument.

Photos: Willard Luce

Scenic panorama is enjoyed by visitors to Dixie National Forest as they stand on Strawberry Point and look across V[i]gin River country to Zion National Par[k]

Sipapu Natural Bridge is the largest and most impressive of the three water-carved bridges comprising Natural Bridg[e] National Monument, in southeastern Uta[h]

286

Photos: U. S. For[est] Service; Willard Lu[ce]

NEVADA MATCHES 24-HOUR GAMBLING AND GREAT SCENIC BEAUTY

Fremont Street, Las Vegas, glories in dancing dice, spinning wheels of fortune.

Pyramid Lake, just 30 miles from Reno, is beautiful blue gem set in the desert.

Photos: TWA Trans World Airlines; Reno Chamber of Commerce

Famous Reno arch across Virginia Street displays slogan that the city tries hard to live up to. Beyond arch are principal hotels, clubs, places of entertainment.

Spectacular sign identifies Harolds Club, nationally known gaming establishment.

Tax on gambling helped build this new modern $3 million high school in Reno.

In this pastoral Reno park, you wouldn't think you were in Nevada's largest city.

University of Nevada has outstanding school of mines and school of journalism.

oulette is one popular form of gambling
Reno and Las Vegas, but there are also
slot machines, poker games, many others.
Players—win or lose—are seldom gay.

to: Henri Cartier-Bresson (Magnum)

Nevada

Virginia City, "richest hill on earth" in 1800's, is perched high on slopes of Sun Mountain. It is now having boom tourists re-living the old bonanza da

Double chair lift at new Reno Ski Bowl carries skiers to height of 9,600 feet.

The Parachutes are interesting formatio in Lehman Caves National Monume

290

Photos: Henri Cartier-Bresson (Magnu Reno Chamber of Commerce; Willard L

orseback riding is enjoyed at many
est ranches near Reno and Las Vegas.

Lake Tahoe, 40 minutes drive from Reno,
is beautiful vacation setting in mountains.

athedral Gorge, state park in eastern
evada, has spectacular stone steeples.

About 87% of Nevada's land is Federally
owned, highest percentage of any state.

ate Capitol is at Carson City, named
r Kit Carson, 24 miles south of Reno.

Among the Indian tribes in Nevada were
the Paiutes, Washoes and Shoshoneans.

Nevada

Hoover Dam, on Colorado River, is used for flood control, irrigation and hydro-electric power. It forms 115-mile La Mead, the largest reservoir in the worl

Elephant Rock is formation in the Valley of Fire, Lake Mead Recreational Area.

Humboldt National Forest is part of fiv million acres of forest reserves in stat

292

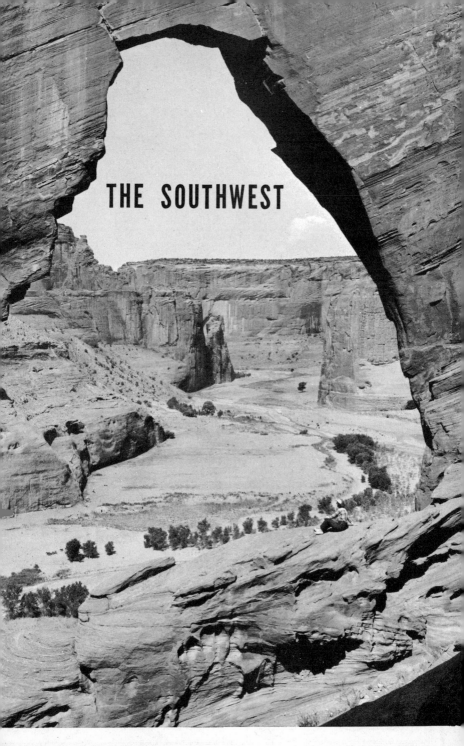

THE SOUTHWEST

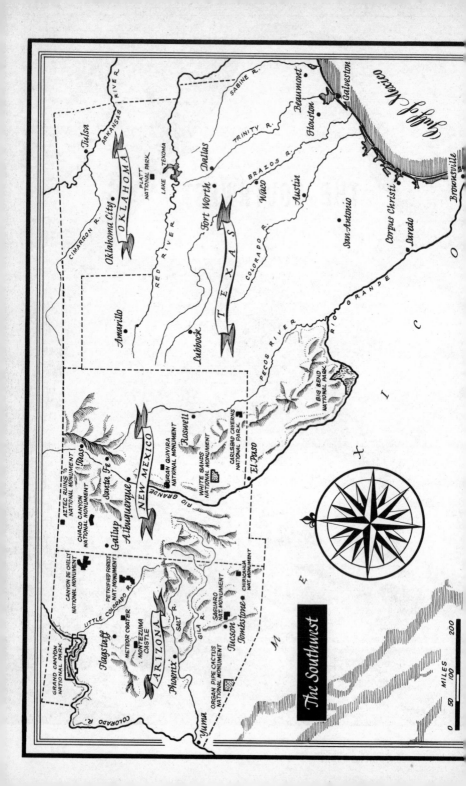

RAND CANYON IS TOP SCENIC LURE
OF ARIZONA'S SUNLAND

rand Canyon of the Colorado is by all
lds the greatest single spectacle in
America. It cuts a 217-mile gash across
Northern Arizona, 4 to 18 miles in width.

oto: Union Pacific Railroad

Arizona

In Monument Valley, giant rock buttes stick up 1200 feet from the valley floor, near the border between Arizona a Utah. Valley also has many sand dun

Saguaro National Monument preserves the giant cactus that serves as a natural storage tank for meager desert rainf Largest specimens grow to 50-foot heig

Organ Pipe Cactus National Monument has 20-foot organ-pipe cacti, other species.

Chiricahua National Monument outdo all others in grotesqueness of its rock

296

Photos: Ray Manley, bottom left, Charles W. H bert (Western Ways); bottom right, Willard L

Mount Lemmon Highway has mantle of now, found only on the higher mountain slopes. Arizona is noted for its many days of sunshine, about 80% of the year.

Montezuma Castle National Monument has remarkable Indian cliff dwellings.

White House, niched into towering walls of Canyon de Chelly, is 900 years old.

Photos: top, Bill Sears, bottom right, Ray Manley (Western Ways); bottom left, TWA Trans World Airlines

Arizona

Vast areas of semi-arid land, suitable only for grazing, make stock-raising an important industry. State has more tha[n] a million head of cattle, even more sheep[.]

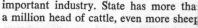

One of a cowboy's duties is to locate a stray calf, bring it home to the ranch.

Cow hand demonstrates roping of calf so it can be branded with Empire mark[.]

Photos: Balestrero, bottom left
Ray Manley (Western Ways

t Desert Willow Ranch, dudes on winter
cation are given a lesson on proper
way to saddle a horse for trail riding. Visitors find crisp desert air invigorating.

offee tastes extra special when it is made
om sparkling mountain stream water.

Note rubber tires on this modern chuck
wagon, vital equipment on working ranch.

huck wagon keeps ahead of moving
erd, provides warm chow at mealtime.

Dudes from Flying V Ranch enjoy evening chow in Santa Catalina Mountains.

Arizona's capital, Phoenix, is lively, friendly city, protected on the north by the Phoenix Mountains. At top right odd silhouette of Camelback Mountai

Camelback Inn is one of elegant Phoenix resorts where life centers around pool.

Phoenix South Mountain Park has ancie writings on stone, and á small gold min

ucson ranks next to Phoenix in size, and
hares its mild, warm dry climate. Both

have much business and industry, but
are best known as tourist, health resorts.

Fiesta and rodeo take place at Tucson
n February, at height of winter season.

Ted DeGrazia, one of Southwest's leading
artists, teaches at his school in Tucson.

Arizona

San Xavier del Bac Mission, consecrated 1797, is considered finest mission architecture in Southwest. This is the mission famous Arizona Boys Chorus at practice

Hopi corn-grinding dance: The Indians of Arizona are divided into more than 30 tribes, the Navajo, Apache, Hopi, Pima Papago, Mojave, Yuma and many others

Tony Whitecloud performs hoop dance at the annual Indian Powwow at Flagstaff.

Navajo woman demonstrates first step i preparing to weave intricate rug desigr

302

Photos: Ray Manley (Western Ways center, Phoenix Chamber of Commerc

Apache Indians take part in Flagstaff Powwow Parade. Indian reservations are near this city which is sheltered by San Francisco Peaks and Elden Mountain.

Tombstone is old mining town which was big boom city of 7,000 in the 1880's, when some of biggest gold mines in state were active. Helldorado Days enact past.

Hoover Dam, shown in different view on page 292, is shared by Northwest Arizona and Southeast Nevada. Called Boulder Dam, 1933–47, it was re-named Hoover.

Arizona

Baldwins Crossing has beautiful red rock in the background. This is popular spot with movie makers who find Arizon fine for shooting with 80% sunny days

Meteor Crater is 600-foot-deep depression believed caused by meteor striking earth.

Painted Desert is large arid area noted for the great variety of its color effects

304

Photos: Valdis Avots; bottom, Frashers Inc., Petrifie
Forest National Park, and National Highway 66 Associatio

CARLSBAD CAVERNS IS TOP
ATTRACTION IN NEW MEXICO

Gargantuan stalagmites and bewildering variety of other formations are seen in Hall of the Giants in Carlsbad Caverns National Park, an underground fairyland.

Photo: New Mexico
State Tourist Bureau

White Sands National Monument has some 176,000 acres of vast, shifting dunes, stretching to the skyline. The dunes are not true sand, but nearly pure gypsum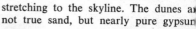

El Morro National Monument preserves rock with 17th century Spanish writings.

Pueblo Bonito is largest of old ruins in Chaco Canyon National Monument

Photos: New Mexico
State Tourist Bureau

Inter-tribal Indian Ceremonial, held each year at Gallup, draws Indians from 31 tribes in the Southwest. They parade in covered wagons, dance and powwow.

Navajo rugs are woven on a crude loom that rests on side of the Indian dwelling.

Beautifully costumed Indian women parade with burdens carried on their heads.

Photos: New Mexico
State Tourist Bureau

New Mexico

Organ Mountains, northeast of Las Cruces: New Mexico varies from 2,876 above sea level to 13,306 feet, a variatio caused by great shiftings of earth's crust

Library at the University of New Mexico, Albuquerque, is constructed in pueblo style architecture and is one of mos beautiful buildings on 315-acre campus

308

tate Capitol in Santa Fe: Distinctive ew building was completed in 1953.

With Palace of Governors, below, state has nation's newest and oldest capitols.

athedral of St. Francis was built in 869 to serve needs of Spanish residents.

Fiesta in Santa Fe is held annually over the three-day Labor Day weekend.

his is America's oldest public building, alace of the Governors, Santa Fe. It

was constructed of adobe, in 1610, and served as State Capitol nearly 300 years.

New Mexico

Mission Church at Pecos Pueblo, now in ruins, was one of largest in the state.

Mission Ranchos de Taos has twin be towers and crosses, beautiful entry doo

Taos Pueblo is spectacular Indian village, with primitive cubist skyscrapers. It is

at foot of the majestic Sangre de Crist mountain range, in northern part of state

Replica of cliff house is seen in Frijoles Canyon, Bandelier National Monument.

Acoma Mission is unique church in Sky City, Indian pueblo 400 feet above plain

310

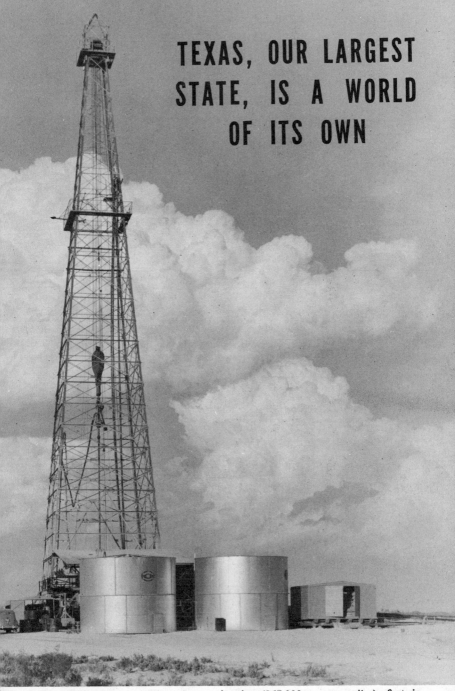

TEXAS, OUR LARGEST STATE, IS A WORLD OF ITS OWN

One of the world's largest drilling rigs, his typifies the bigness of Texas, first in size (267,339 square miles), first in oil production and in many farm products.

Houston is the largest city in the Lone
Star State, big manufacturing center and
one of greatest U.S. ports, with 50-mi
canal to Gulf. Shamrock Hotel is at le[ft]

Shamrock, in Eastern Panhandle section,
is home of the annual St. Patrick's Day
celebration, and of the Eastern Panhandl[e]
Livestock Show fourth week in February

Photos: Braniff International Airway[s]
National Highway 66 Associati[on]

Texas State Capitol, at Austin, has 18 acres of floor space and some 500 rooms. Built of native red granite, it is 308 ft. high, topping most other state capitols.

State Fair of Texas, held at Dallas in October, is largest of its kind in the nation, drawing over 2½ million attendance. In background is Hall of State Building.

Photos: Texas Highway Department; Braniff International Airways

Corpus Christi Bay and skyline of city: Sheltered from Gulf of Mexico by Mustang Island, Corpus Christi is shipping center and all-year-round playground

Alabama-Cooshatti Indians, only remaining tribe in Texas, live near Livingston.

Arthur's, in Dallas, is one of the state's distinguished places for excellent food.

Galveston's long beach for surf bathing, good climate, facilities for fishing and boating, attractive subtropical plants, all combine to make it tourist playground.

Photos: Texas Highway Department; center right, Arthur's

San Antonio River flows through lovely park in downtown San Antonio. One of oldest Texas cities, and third largest, it has interesting past, colorful present.

The Alamo, where heroic defenders died, is one of best-known U.S. historic shrines.

Spanish Governors' Palace, San Antonio, was used during Spanish rule of Texas.

McDonald Observatory, located in Dav
Mountains, is third largest in the worl

Indian Lodge is tourist resort in Davi
Mountains, towering to 7,000-foot peaks

570-foot San Jacinto Monument commemorates battle for Texas freedom.

Spring roundup is like a three ring circus
—you have to be quick to see everything.

This typical scene is near Vernon, which
has one livestock pasture of 200,000 acres

Mission San José is the most complete of the four Spanish missions standing in San Antonio. Established 1720, it was most beautiful, prosperous in New Spain.

Church of Our Lady of Mount Carmel is reproduction of mission founded in 1681.

At Mission Espíritu Santo, in Goliad, excavators found ancient Indian homes.

Photos: Texas Highway Department; bottom left, Ray Manley (Western Ways)

Judge Roy Bean Museum preserves memory of Justice of Peace, his colorful era.

Roadside park gives view of El Capitan and Guadalupe Peak, highest in state.

Palo Duro Canyon State Park has many beautiful vistas, often attainable only by

Santa Elena Canyon, Big Bend Park, is one of the Rio Grande's three deepest.

Mansfield Dam, high as 25-story building, forms beautiful 65-mile-long Lake Travis

horseback. There are 50 miles of bridle paths in the 15,103-acre park. Hiking trails are plentiful; their winding routes give delightful view of multicolored walls.

Balmorhea State Park, in Davis Mountains, boasts a spring-fed swimming pool.

This is replica of Old Stone Fort, rebuilt at Stephen F. Austin State College.

Photos: Texas State Highway Department

Texas

Purchasing colorful and serviceable boot is vital shopping-day task for cowboys

Christo Rey: This monument to Prince of Peace is on summit in northwest El Paso.

Historic field piece stands near first o the Hilton Hotels, in downtown El Paso

International bridge crosses Rio Grande from Juarez, Mexico, to El Paso, the city that stands at westernmost tip of Texas. Name means "the Pass" through hills.

Photos: Ray Manley, top right, C. W. Herbert (Western Ways)

OKLAHOMA POSSESSES GREAT RICHES, GREAT CAPACITY TO ENJOY THEM

Oklahoma City, capital of the state, has symbols of its wealth—a row of oil wells —right on the State House grounds. City was settled in one day, by homesteaders.

Oklahoma

Turner Falls, in the Arbuckle Mountains near Davis, is one of the scenic spots of Oklahoma. The state has four mounta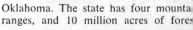 ranges, and 10 million acres of fores

Platt National Park, near Sulphur, in the southern part of state, has streams, springs, waterfalls, swimming holes. was once part of old Indian Territory

Photos: Charles J. Belden; National Par Service; Oklahoma Planning & Resources Boar

klahoma Agricultural and Mechanical ollege, at Stillwater, was founded 1890.

It has $50 million in buildings, equipment, 4,976 acres of land, 8,800 students.

niversity of Oklahoma, at Norman, has rollment of 8,000, and 2,471 acres of

land. University of Oklahoma Press is noted for success of regional publishing.

Vill Rogers Memorial at Claremore honrs the Oklahoma humorist-philosopher.

Indian population is largest of any state, comprising members of some thirty tribes.

hotos: Oklahoma Planning & Resources Board; bottom, laremore Chamber of Commerce; El Reno Chamber f Commerce, and National Highway 66 Association

323

Oklahoma

Lake Texoma, shared by Oklahoma, Texas, is one of our biggest playgrounds.

Cimarron and many other rivers in th state provide abundant fishing stream

Devils Den is quiet spot created by some angry upheaval of the earth's crust

centuries ago. Now it's ideal for rocl clambering and just plain contemplatio

Lake o' the Cherokees is formed by huge multiple-arch Grand River Dam, built in

1938–41, and also called the Pensacol Dam. The lake covers 85 square mile

324

CALIFORNIA—THE GOLDEN GATE

Photo: Yosemite National
Park, by Western Ways

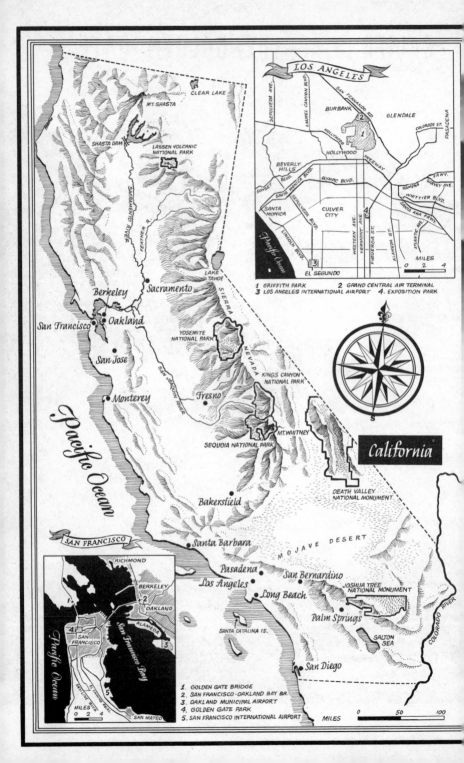

California

LOS ANGELES

1 GRIFFITH PARK   2 GRAND CENTRAL AIR TERMINAL
3 LOS ANGELES INTERNATIONAL AIRPORT   4 EXPOSITION PARK

SAN FRANCISCO

1. GOLDEN GATE BRIDGE
2. SAN FRANCISCO-OAKLAND BAY BR.
3. OAKLAND MUNICIPAL AIRPORT
4. GOLDEN GATE PARK
5. SAN FRANCISCO INTERNATIONAL AIRPORT

YOSEMITE PARK HEADS THE NATURAL WONDERS OF NORTHERN CALIFORNIA

Yosemite National Park is a peaceful empire of 1,189 square miles, with giant sequoias, tumbling waterfalls, and lakes which reflect the spectacular mountains.

Photo: Konstantin Kostich

Yosemite Valley is in the heart of the great national park's scenic marvels, with Half Dome looming ahead. Park lies on western slope of the Sierra Nevada

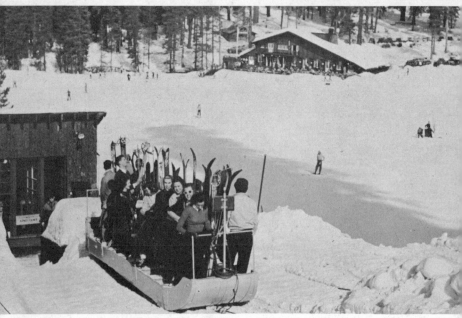

Ski-tow at Yosemite is sort of uphill sled. National parks and many other places provide Californians with tobogganing snowshoeing, skiing, sleighing, ice-skating

Photos: Southern Pacific
Lines; Konstantin Kostic

Yosemite Fall first leaps a sheer 1,430 feet and then, after a series of cascades, plunges another 320. Park has five great falls, one 10 times height of Niagara.

Photo: United Air Lines

329

San Francisco, with its roller-coaster streets, ranks with Paris and Rome as one of world's greatly loved cities. Cable cars have won fight to keep clanging

"**Top of the Mark**" is the many-windowed antage point where San Franciscans and visitors meet for cocktails while they watch the great city spread out below.

Mark Hopkins Hotel is built on Nob Hill, where railroad-builder's mansion stood.

Ferry Building, foot of Market Street, is less active because of Bay Bridge.

Photos: Henri Cartier-Bresson (Magnum); bottom left, Moulin Studios; right, Redwood Empire Association

This air view shows San Francisco from the Civic Center, in center foreground, to the docks. In distance is San Francisco Bay, with the 8¼-mile-long San Fran-

cisco-Oakland Bay Bridge, which passes through Yerba Buena Island in mid-bay by means of a tunnel. On far shore are East Bay cities of Oakland, Berkeley.

Golden Gate Bridge, connecting San Francisco with communities to the north, was completed in 1937 at cost of $35½ million. Main central span, 4,200 feet

Fisherman's Wharf is landing point for San Francisco's many Italian fishermen. Visitors love brightly painted fishing boats, and many fine seafood restaurants.

n length, is the longest single span in
he world. The bridge carries 6 lanes for
auto traffic, has 2 sidewalks. Clearance
above San Francisco Bay is 220 feet.

Sidewalk stands on Wharf cook freshly
caught crabs in steaming iron cauldrons.

San Francisco's Chinatown is an exotic
city-within-a-city of more than 20,000.

San Francisco-Oakland Bay Bridge was opened to traffic in 1936. It is double-decked, with six traffic lanes for auto on the upper level, and three truck lanes

Mission Dolores, in downtown San Francisco, was founded on June 29, 1776.

Trader Vic's, with main restaurant i San Francisco and one in Oakland, i

336

nd two interurban tracks on the lower. he bridge is illuminated at night with yellow sodium vapor lights, the rays of which can penetrate the frequent fogs.

ne of bay area's many notable eating laces. Vic's has South Seas atmosphere.

Unique cable cars were doomed to oblivion, but aroused public saved many.

Photos: Strohmeyer Photographs; bottom left, Californians Inc.; enter, Trader Vic's; San Francisco Chamber of Commerce

California THE GOLDEN GATE

Union Square, San Francisco: At left is St. Francis Hotel, one of best known.

Beneath square is four-level garage with capacity for more than 1,700 automobiles

San Francisco meets the Pacific on long white beach extending over 3½ miles.

Outdoor flower stands are to Union Square what cafés are to Champs-Elysées

Photos: Californians Inc.; bottom right, Redwood Empire Association

...ther Gate is famed entrance to the ...niversity of California at Berkeley.

Campanile's high lookout gives splendid view of San Francisco and whole bay area.

...rader Vic's in Oakland is even more ...outh Seas than San Francisco version.

Hoover Tower, at Stanford University, houses library on war, revolution, peace.

Lake Tahoe, shared by Nevada, California, is of glacial origin and covers nearly 200 square miles. Mark Twain called "fairest picture the whole earth afford

Sutter's Fort, in California's capital city of Sacramento, contains authentic exhibits showing life in the early day and during the hectic Gold Rush perio

340

assen Peak is the only recently active olcano in the United States. Violent eruptions occurred in 1914 and 1915, after sixty-five years of inactivity.

California THE GOLDEN GATE

This is the rugged coast along Del Norte County, near boundary of Oregon. Area from San Francisco north to the Oregon border is known as the Redwood Empire

In Eldorado National Forest, a "shovel" loader places huge logs on truck. Except for its valuable redwoods, California must import much of the lumber it needs

Photos: Redwood Empire Association; U. S. Forest Service

hese Giant Sequoias in Mariposa Grove,
osemite National Park, are probably the
oldest living things in the world. Ring
counts show some to be 4,000 years old.

The Napa, Livermore and Sonoma valleys produce grapes for table use, raisins 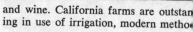 and wine. California farms are outstanding in use of irrigation, modern method

California wineries make about 90% of the country's domestic wines, brandies.

Blossomtime in Santa Clara Valley: It called "Valley of the heart's delight.

Photos: Redwood Empire Association; bottom right, San Jose Chamber of Commerce

SOUTHERN CALIFORNIA

Photo: Joshua Tree National Monument,
by Charles W. Herbert (Western Ways)

SOUTHERN CALIFORNIA MEANS HOLLYWOOD, ORANGE GROVES, COAST AND DESERT RESORTS

Palm Springs, in the desert 70 miles southeast of Los Angeles, is an opulent resort that is said to have the world's highest per capita count of swimming pool

Photos: Charles Herbert (Western Way

Hollywood is center of world's movie industry. Hollywood Boulevard becomes "Santa Claus Lane" at Christmas and is gaily festooned, brilliantly floodlighted.

Grauman's Chinese Theater is noted for glamorous movie premieres and for the concrete slabs bearing hand and foot prints and messages from celebrities.

Photos: Hollywood Citizen-News; Hollywood Chamber of Commerce

Southern California LOS ANGELES

Wilshire Boulevard, famous Los Angeles thoroughfare, sweeps through MacArthur Park and on to the Miracle Mile section with spectacular shops, hotels, office

New Chinatown is Los Angeles center for curio shops and Oriental restaurants.

Union Station, in modified mission architecture, has 135-foot clock tower

348

Photos: TWA Trans World Airlines; Konstanti Kostich; All Year Club of Southern Californi

Biltmore Hotel is on edge of Pershing Square in heart of downtown Los Angeles.

A multi-level garage has recently been constructed beneath the palm-lined park.

Guests at Beverly Wilshire enjoy lunch beside the big "Copa Club" swimming pool.

Fashion shows, fencing exhibitions are among events attracting crowds to hotel.

The famous Rose Bowl, at Pasadena, is packed with nearly 100,000 fans on each New Year's Day to see the keen rivalry of the annual Rose Bowl football game

Santa Anita Race Track, with mountains as backdrop, is one of handsomest. Mid-winter racing events attract throngs to $1 million plant with stands for 30,000.

350

Redlands, named for red soil of region, is packing and distributing center for wide citrus growing area. It is protected on the north by San Bernardino Mountains.

Lake Arrowhead, a mile high in the San Bernardino Mountains, is reached by scenic Rim of the World Drive, a 100-mile loop from San Bernardino and return.

Photos: Redlands Chamber of Commerce; TWA Trans World Airlines

San Diego has one of the finest natural harbors in the U.S., attracting naval, commercial and pleasure craft. Growi industries have given population big boo

Serra Museum, of Spanish mission design, honors days of Father Junípero Serra.

Tower of California Building, in Balb Park, is outstanding San Diego landmar

352

a Jolla, just north of San Diego, has
vely homes on cliffs overlooking the sea.

Alligator Head, secluded sandy cove, is
La Jolla's most popular spot for bathing.

he coves, headlands and flower-covered
aths of Laguna Beach have served as in-

spiration for many landscape painters. The
town has many rustic homes and shops.

Rodeo Parade at Palm Springs attracts gay-costumed riders from ranches for many miles around. Other events inclu golf and tennis tournaments, circus we

Youthful rider shows her skill in parade that passes along Palm Springs main street.

Young horse, too, puts on his best manne for event sponsored by Mounted Polic

Photos: A. Milton Runy

Palm Springs Tennis Club is a beautiful oasis in the desert Its swimming pool is one of well over 1,000 in Palm Springs, probably world's highest per-person count.

Photo: Charles W. Herbert (Western Ways)

Dante's View overlooks Death Valley from the summit of the Black Mountains.

You can see Mt. Whitney and Badwat the highest and the lowest points in U.

Close-up shows steep, rugged mountain walls that baffled the Death Valley party

of 1849. The valley has white salt area gravel slopes, green patches of mesquit

Photos: TWA Trans World Airline
Charles W. Herbert (Western Ways

Mt. Whitney from the air: With elevation of 14,495 feet, this peak of the Sierra Nevada is highest in U.S. It was named after Josiah Dwight Whitney, geologist.

Joshua Tree National Monument contains this odd Wonderland of Rocks, and many of the Joshua trees (*Yucca arborescens*) peculiar to the Mojave Desert region.

Photos: American Airlines; All Year Club of Southern California

357

Palisade Glaciers, near Big Pine, are the southernmost of the Northern Hemi-

sphere. The gleaming "living ice" is tw‹ miles long, a mile wide, deeply crevassed

Photo: American Airline‹

General Sherman Tree, Sequoia-King's Canyon National Park, is *Sequoia gigantea.*

Sierra Nevada Mountains form eastern boundary of King's Canyon National Park.

Close-up of comely lass in Giant Joshua Tree: These desert lilies often grow 30 feet high and 3 feet thick. A forest of them covers desert area near Palmdale.

Photos: Southern Pacific; Ansel Adams;
All Year Club of Southern California

Santa Barbara, founded 1786, is called "Queen of the Missions." It is the only California mission whose altar light has never been extinguished since founding

Mission San Gabriel was founded in 1771 by the pioneer missionary, Junípero Serra.

Mission St. Charles Borromeo overlooks Carmel Bay. It has grave of Father Serra.

Mission Santa Ynez prospered in 1820, at which time it owned 12,000 head of cattle.

Mission San Diego de Alcalá was first of the 21 missions built by the Franciscans.

Southern California OIL AND AGRICULTURE

California ranks next to Texas in crude petroleum production. This is the valley where most of the rigs of the Ventura field stand, pumping black gold night and day

Typical pumping unit in the oil fields is this conventional rocker-arm type of pump.

Oilmen tackling a new field have to slice mountains, bulldoze roads, haul in rigs.

Date clusters are covered with burlap or paper cones while the fruit is ripening.

Orange growing in California is world's most intensively-developed crop culture.

Abundance of water from melting snows of the Sierra Nevada, together with long

hot summers, helps make the San Joaquin Valley vineyards a vast green garden.

Wine is stored in these huge barrels. Man on ladder uses "thief" to draw sample.

Cotton production centers on Alcalá, a quality variety that is in great demand.

Photos: All Year Club of Southern California; Wine Institute; Kern County Board of Trade

Southern California

Cabrillo Boulevard, Santa Barbara: To the right is the municipal swimming pool and the Santa Barbara channel. To the left is the city and Santa Ynez Mountains

Santa Barbara's white stucco courthouse resembles palace of a Spanish prelate.

Pigeons and swallows make their home in ruins of old Mission San Juan Capistrano.

Santa Catalina Island is 24 miles southwest of Los Angeles harbor. Avalon is the main center of this glamorous sport and resort showplace. Casino is at right.

Photos: Santa Barbara Chamber of Commerce; All Year Club of Southern California; Southern Pacific

THE NORTHWEST

Photo: Sheep Rock, Oregon, by
Oregon State Highway Commission

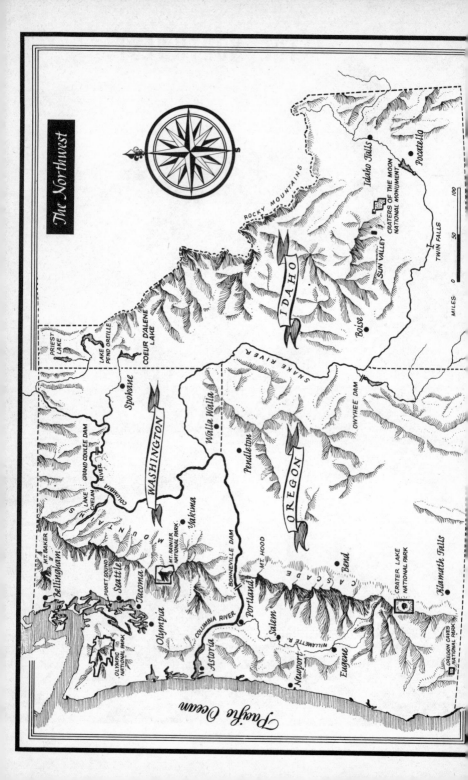

SUN VALLEY IS GLAMOR RESORT
OF MAGNIFICENTLY RUGGED IDAHO

At Sun Valley, snow falls deep and powdery from early autumn on, the sun shines brilliantly, and the Sawtooth Mountains give protection from cold northern gales.

Sun Valley Lodge offers ice skating, the thrilling ski runs of Mount Baldy, milder slopes of Dollar and Half Dollar Mountains, even swimming in heated pools.

Photo: Sun Valley News Bureau

Sun Valley is year-round resort. Fishing for rainbow trout is favorite summer sport.

Boise is Idaho's capital and largest city, with its monumentally classic capitol.

Craters of the Moon National Monument: The splatter cones, terraces and weird piles of stone, caves and natural bridges resemble the moon seen through a telescope.

Indians say a dip before sunrise at Bathtub Rock will restore youth to the aged.

Thousand Springs gush forth from the lava edges and plunge down into Snake River.

Idaho

Trail Riders explore the wilderness in Idaho's Primitive Area, a million-acre land of mountains and streams, plateaus and ridges, meadows, four National Forests

Shoshone Falls is largest of the Snake River waterfalls, a thousand feet across its horseshoe curve and 212 feet deep. Irrigation dams make the flow irregular

Photos: Ross Madden (Western Ways); Willard Luc

CRATER LAKE AND CASCADE RANGE
FEATURE OREGON'S RUGGED GRANDEUR

Mt. Hood loop, a wide, paved highway, encircles Oregon's highest peak, 11,245-ft.

Mt. Hood is in the imposing Cascade Range. Rhododendrons grow on slopes.

Photo: Oregon State
Highway Commission

Oregon

Portland is Oregon's largest city with more than a half million in the urban area.

This view is from Washington Park, with Mt. Hood in the distance, 50 miles away.

Known as "City of Roses," Portland has Rose Festival in June, with Floral Parade.

International rose test gardens cover a large acreage in city's Washington Park

372

"Joaquin Miller Chapel" is seen on the guided tour through famous Oregon Caves.

Pioneer figure atop Capitol at Salem symbolizes westward march of settlers.

Bachelor Butte is the predominant peak seen from Todd Lake and meadows, west of Bend. The lake is a favorite trout fishing spot in the central Oregon area.

Gladioli are an important flower crop in Grants Pass region, Josephine County.

Indian maiden displays her costume at the Pendleton Round-Up in eastern Oregon.

At Crater Lake National Park, visitors are looking toward Wizard Island, a small lava cone that rises 700 feet high out o the water of this mysterious blue lake

Astoria's fishing fleet waits for run of salmon to hit Columbia River or the coast.

Ancient Indian writings are found on roc cliffs of Picture Gorge, near Dayville

Photos: Oregon Stat
Highway Commissio

Vista House lookout, atop Crown Point, gives this view of Columbia River Gorge and the scenic path the mighty river has swept out through the Cascade Mountains.

Bonneville Dam, built 1933–43, is one of the Northwest's hydroelectric giants.

Fish ladders enable salmon to circumvent dam and swim upriver to spawning grounds.

Norwegian freighter docks at Coos Bay, one of coast's great lumber shipping ports.

Old fort at The Dalles displays many items pioneers brought in covered wagons.

Photos: Oregon State Highway Commission; top, Northwest Orient Airlines

Oregon

Winter brings a snowy white mantle to Mt. Hood and the trees at timberline.

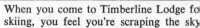

When you come to Timberline Lodge fo skiing, you feel you're scraping the sky

Oregon Caves Chateau is near entrance to the spectacular underground Marble Halls.

Baker's First National Bank displays multimillion dollar collection of gold

Seal Rock State Park, south of Newport, is good place to view wild and color-

ful Oregon coast. Seals may frequentl be seen on rocks beyond the breakers

Photos: Oregon State Highway Commis sion; top, Northwest Orient Airline

WASHINGTON'S BOLD FEATURES OFFER SOME OF WORLD'S LOVELIEST SCENES

Majestic Mount Rainier is the 14,408-ft. peak that the Indians called God. Clear water of Reflection Lake mirrors snow-crowned top of state's highest mountain.

Photo: Northern Pacific Railway

Hikers tackle the slopes of Mt. Rainier close to timberline. On a clear day you can see the Cascades billowing north to British Columbia, south toward California.

Olympic National Park includes nearly 850,000 acres, with most of the major peaks of the Olympic Mountains. This is Mt. Olympus, from Hurricane Ridge Road.

Photos: top, Northwest Orient Airlines; Washington State Advertising Commission

Seattle's crowded skyline testifies to its importance as Washington's largest city (620,000 in the urban area) and as world port, transcontinental rail terminus.

Floating bridge is unique feature of Lake Washington, within Seattle city limits.

Government locks connect Puget Sound with Seattle's inland lakes and canals.

A young visitor to Washington studies the variety of boats docked at Westport, on sheltered Grays Harbor. Evergreen State has lakes, rivers, ocean, and inland sea.

Photos: Washington State Advertising Commission

Spokane is hub of the Inland Empire, the vast northwest area that produces wheat, apples, lumber. A pioneer trading post in 1872, it's now second city in the state.

Mt. Spokane is center of 3,000-acre state park. This view shows Mt. Kit Carson.

Lookout on top of 5,878-ft. Mt. Spokane gives splendid view of eastern Washington.

Gold Creek in Chelan National Forest shows the rugged nature of this region.

Olympia, state capital of Washington, is the southernmost port of Puget Sound.

Grand Coulee Dam, finished 1942, is the largest concrete dam in the world. Water from reservoir flows to farms through a 4,000-mile system of irrigation ditches.

Toppenish is headquarters of the Yakima Indian Agency. This is July 4th pow-wow.

Fishing at Long Beach: This is claimed to be the longest in the world—28 miles.

Tacoma's Fort Nisqually, built by Hudson's Bay Company, was a trading post.

Apples from Yakima and Wenatchee, "Apple Capital of the World," are famous.

Washington

Spirit Lake, at foot of Mount St. Helens, is 44 miles from Castle Rock over a new highway. It has a Forest Service camping ground, excellent trout fishing, hunting.

Truck-trailers, trains and rivers bring Douglas fir and other woods to the mills.

Sheep graze in Gifford Pinchot National Forest, with Mount Adams in background.

This combine is working on pea harvest which now exceeds the value of wheat in many Washington counties. The state also raises barley, oats, potatoes, corn, hops.

Photos: U. S. Forest Service; center left, Washington State Advertising Commission; bottom, Northwest Orient Airlines

INDEX

NATIONAL PARKS

AND MONUMENTS

A DIRECTORY OF U.S. NATIONAL PARKS AND MONUMENTS

NATIONAL PARKS

Acadia, in southern Maine, has 30,378 acres of woodland, lakes, highlands and seashore. Much of the park is on Mount Desert Island. Another section is on the mainland, covering picturesque Schoodic Point, south of Winter Harbor.

Big Bend, in western Texas, known for its abrupt mountain belts and colorful desert, takes its name from its location in the great U-shaped bend of the Rio Grande. Spectacular mountains, canyons and desert plains include a variety of unusual geologic structures. Area of the park is 692,304 acres.

Bryce Canyon, in southwestern Utah, is not really a canyon, but a great horseshoe-shaped bowl or amphitheater cut by water erosion. Bryce's 36,010 acres contain some of the most interesting exposures of the Pink Cliffs formation, among the most colorful of rocks forming the earth's crust.

Carlsbad Caverns, in southeastern New Mexico, is a labyrinth of underground caverns, many of huge size, with curious natural formations. The park has been enlarged to 45,846 acres. Development of the caves has been limited to the 750-ft. and 829-ft. levels reached by trail from the natural entrance and by elevator.

Photo: Bryce Canyon National Park, by Hubert A. Lowman

Crater Lake, in southwestern Oregon, features an unbelievably blue body of water in the crater of a great volcano, mighty Mount Mazama. This is the focal point of the 160,290-acre park, on the crest of the Cascade Range.

Everglades, in southern Florida, is our third largest park, with 1,500,000 acres of saw-grass prairies, mangrove forests, and marshes. The largest remaining subtropical wilderness in the U.S., it abounds in wildlife, with many of the spectacular wading birds, such as egrets, ibis, herons, spoonbills. Guided trips by boat may be made during the winter season.

Glacier, lying athwart the Rocky Mountains of northwestern Montana, contains almost one million acres of the most gloriously scenic portions of the whole range. Its 60 glaciers are among the few in the U.S. that are easily accessible. There are 200 beautiful lakes. International Peace Park, which includes this park and Canada's Waterton Lakes National Park, was established in 1932.

Grand Canyon, in northwestern Arizona, is the tremendous mile-deep gorge of the Colorado River, varying in width from 4 to 18 miles. The canyon is 217 miles long, with 105 miles of that distance within the park's 673,062 acres. The fantastically colored formations and rock masses make the Grand Canyon one of the world's greatest wonders.

Grand Teton, in northwestern Wyoming, includes the most scenic portion of the majestic Teton Mountain Range, and the northern portion of Jackson Hole, a high mountain valley famous for its associations with early western history. Enlarged in 1950, the park now contains approximately 300,000 acres.

Great Smoky Mountains, located on the crest of the high divide which forms the boundary between Tennessee and North Carolina, takes its name from the deep blue haze rising from the valleys to the summits of the lofty peaks. Loftiest range

Photo: Great Smoky Mountains National Park, by E. D. DePew

east of the Black Hills, the Great Smokies boast 16 peaks over 6,000 feet high. This wild, beautiful area, because of its accessibility to major cities, is one of our most widely visited parks. Its area is 507,168 acres.

Hawaii National Park contains 176,950 acres in two separate areas, the Kilauea-Mauna Loa section, on the island of Hawaii, and the Haleakala section, on the island of Maui. This spectacular volcanic region contains two volcanoes in frequent eruption, luxuriant tropical forests, native birds, cliffs, rugged coastline.

Hot Springs National Park and the adjoining city of Hot Springs are near the center of Arkansas, 50 miles southwest of Little Rock. The park contains about 1,000 acres in a picturesquely wooded section of the Ouachita (Wash-i-taw) Mountains, with 47 hot springs whose waters are considered to have therapeutic effects.

Isle Royale is unique among our 28 national parks in its wilderness setting, isolated as it is from the mainland of northern Michigan by many miles of Lake Superior waters. The main island, largest in the lake, is surrounded by 200 small islands. Moose are commonly seen near the water, and more than 200 kinds of birds have been listed. Isle Royale Park has 133,838 acres.

Kings Canyon is discussed under the adjoining Sequoia National Park, see p. 393.

Lassen Volcanic National Park, in northeastern California, preserves Lassen Peak, at the southern end of the Cascade Range. The only recently active peak in the U.S. proper, its latest eruptions occurred between 1914 and 1917. The peak is 10,453 feet high and is almost completely wrapped in a mantle of rock fragments broken from its own great cliffs. Park has 104,160 acres.

Mammoth Cave, in southern Kentucky, has long been considered one of the seven

wonders of the New World, and has been attracting visitors for nearly a century and a half. The park embraces 50,695 surface acres, but the interest of visitors is concentrated on the underground caves and passages with their beautiful limestone formations. Echo River is 360 feet below the surface, and famous Crystal Lake is 270 feet underground. The cave has four main entrances.

Mesa Verde, in southwestern Colorado, preserves the ruins of hundreds of dwellings which prehistoric Indians built on the mesa tops and the caves of a score of rugged canyons. Spruce Tree House is the best-preserved of the cliff dwellings, and Cliff Palace the largest. The park contains 51,017 acres. The name Mesa Verde is Spanish for "green table," an appropriate name for this land which rises high above the surrounding country.

Mount McKinley National Park, in central Alaska, is our second largest park, with nearly 2 million acres. The principal scenic feature is mighty Mount McKinley, 20,269 feet, the highest peak on the North American continent. The huge park has three other high peaks, many great glaciers.

Photo: Balcony House Ruin, Mesa Verde National Park, by Ansel F. Hall

Mount Rainier, 14,408 feet high, is the superb landmark of Mount Rainier National Park, in the southwestern part of central Washington. Some 26 active glaciers make up the greatest single-peak glacial system in the United States. The mountain covers about one-fourth of the park's 241,571 acres, and there are flower-covered meadows and deep forests.

Olympic National Park, on the Olympic Peninsula of northwestern Washington, is

springs, called Antelope and Buffalo, together flow more than 5 million gallons of pure water a day.

Rocky Mountain National Park, in north-central Colorado, assures preservation of 254,575 acres of the Front Range of the Rocky Mountains. Within the park are 65 named peaks more than 10,000 feet high, the highest being 14,255-ft. Longs Peak. Two routes offer the mountain climber access to its summit, and the park offers

a unique wilderness containing 888,182 acres of rugged mountains, coniferous rain forests, wildlife, glaciers, lakes, streams, and seascapes. Some 4,000 elk live in the park. Mount Olympus, highest peak of the Olympic Mountains, is 7,954 feet high. Precipitation in the mountains is as much as 200 inches a year.

Platt, in southern Oklahoma, contains 911 acres of cold mineral springs, some of sulphur and some of bromide. The springs are located in the valleys along Travertine and Rock Creeks. Two natural

many climbs, varying from easy trail trips to difficult technical ascents. Three scenic highways give wonderful views of forested canyons, lake-studded gorges, lofty peaks.

Sequoia and Kings Canyon National Parks lie across the heart of the Sierra Nevada in eastern central California. The borders extend from the foothills of the San Joaquin Valley to the crest of the High Sierra, and between these extremes of elevation is a great variety of natural scenic features and wildlife. Sequoia con-

Photo: Cliff Palace Ruin, Mesa Verde National Park, by Ansel F. Hall

Photo: Giant Sequoias in California's Redwood Empire, by Ray Atkeson

tains 385,178 acres, Kings Canyon 453,-
064. Best known feature of Sequoia is the
Giant Forest, containing the General
Sherman Tree, the largest and possibly
the oldest of living trees. 272 feet tall,
it is believed 3,500 years old. General
Grant Grove area, in Kings Canyon Park,
has as its chief attraction the General
Grant tree, 267 feet high, second only
to the General Sherman. The Kings River
Canyon itself is a titanic setting, with
huge domes along the canyon wall, over
2,000 feet high, flanked by towering peaks
that rise to a mile or more above the
canyon's brinks. The final feature of
these parks is the wilderness area, the
"back country" region of mountains,
lakes, forests, canyons, streams, meadows.
On the crest of the Sierra Nevada is
Mount Whitney, 14,495 feet, the highest
point in the United States proper.

Shenandoah National Park, in northern
Virginia, extends from Front Royal on
the north to the vicinity of Waynesboro.
The park contains 193,472 acres in the
highest and most scenic section of the
northern Blue Ridge range. Skyline Drive
traverses the entire length of the park
along the crest of the mountains for a distance of 105 miles. Many overlooks afford views of the breathtaking panoramas
of hills, oak forests and meadowland.
Wildflowers bloom from mid-April to
early November.

Wind Cave, in southwestern South Dakota, is a limestone cavern, with beautiful
boxwork and calcite crystal formations.
The cave takes its name from the strong
winds that blow alternately in and out of
the mouth. The park consists of 27,886
acres on the southeast flank of the Black
Hills. Buffalo, antelope and elk are often
seen.

Yellowstone National Park lies in the ex-
treme northwest corner of Wyoming. It
includes within its borders small portions
of Idaho and Montana. It is the largest
and oldest of our national parks, established on March 1, 1872, and with an
area of 2,213,206 acres. A part of the

high country of the middle Rocky Mountains, it contains geysers, hot springs and other thermal features which are the result of volcanic activities prevailing in the area for ages. The geysers are known the world over. Some, like Old Faithful, Daisy and Riverside, erupt at regular intervals; others are irregular. Altogether, there are some 10,000 separate and distinct thermal features. Yellowstone Lake is the largest body of water in North America at so high an altitude—7,731 feet above sea level. The Grand Canyon of the Yellowstone is one of the park's most beautiful areas. The Lower Falls is nearly twice the height of Niagara, 308 feet. Upper Falls drops 109 feet, and Tower Falls plunges 132 feet over rugged boulders. Yellowstone is one of the largest wildlife sanctuaries in the world, with bear, deer, elk, antelope, mountain sheep, coyote, moose and buffalo.

Yosemite National Park, in central California near the Nevada border, is known for its matchless scenery, with waterfalls that can be duplicated nowhere else in the world. The Upper Yosemite Fall drops 1,430 feet in one sheer fall, a height equal to approximately 9 Niagara Falls. The Lower Yosemite Fall has a drop of 320 feet, or two Niagaras more. Counting the series of cascades between, the total drop is 2,425 feet. Ribbon and Bridalveil are the best known of the five other falls. Glacier Point affords a magnificent view of the High Sierra, dominated by 4,852-ft. Half Dome, and looking down into Yosemite Valley, 3,254 feet below. The Mariposa Grove of giant sequoias is another point of interest. The park, including Yosemite Valley and the Mariposa Grove, contains 757,617 acres.

Zion National Park, in the heart of the spectacular desert and canyon country of southwestern Utah, has as one of its chief features the great multicolored gorge, Zion Canyon. It is the vivid coloring of the sandstone cliffs that most amazes. Two thirds of the way up the walls are varying shades of red, then they rise in startling white, sometimes surmounted by a brilliant cap of red. Zion-Mount Carmel Highway runs 11½ miles through the park, and there are 20 miles of roads and 26 miles of trails, some easy and some difficult. The park contains 94,241 acres.

Photos: Zion National Park, by Hubert A. Lowman and Josef Muench

Photo: Fishing Bridge on Yellowstone River, Yellowstone National Park, by Josef Muench

Photo: Nevada Fall, Yosemite National Park, by Ansel Adams

NATIONAL HISTORICAL PARKS

Abraham Lincoln, in central Kentucky near Hodgenville, contains the log cabin believed to be that in which Lincoln was born, in a protective memorial building.

Appomattox Court House, in central Virginia, was historic spot where General Robert E. Lee surrendered to General Ulysses S. Grant to end the Civil War. Established as National Monument in 1940, it was made a National Historical Park in 1954.

Chalmette, in southeastern Louisiana, commemorates the battle of New Orleans, in which Andrew Jackson won from the British the greatest American land victory of the War of 1812.

Colonial, in southeastern Virginia, includes Yorktown, scene of the American victory over Cornwallis in 1781 and the culmination of the American Revolution, Jamestown, Cape Henry Memorial, and Colonial Parkway from Yorktown to Colonial Williamsburg.

Cumberland Gap is the most recent, established September 14, 1955, and the largest historical park in the U.S. Kentucky contributed 10,700 acres, Virginia 7,400 and Tennessee 2,000. The main path through the mountains during the westward movement, Cumberland Gap was known as the "Wilderness Road" in Daniel Boone's day.

Morristown, in northern New Jersey, was site of Washington's military headquarters and the main encampment of his Continental Army during winters of 1777 and 1779–80.

Saratoga, in eastern New York, was scene of the decisive American victory over Burgoyne, 1777, marking the turning point of the American Revolution.

NATIONAL MONUMENTS

Ackia Battleground, in northeastern Mississippi, saw the victory of Chickasaw Indians and English over the French and their Choctaw allies, May 26, 1736.

Andrew Johnson, in Greenville, northeastern Tennessee, contains President Johnson's home, tailor shop, and grave.

Arches, in eastern Utah near Moab, has gigantic but graceful arches in the red sandstone of the "slickrock" country.

Aztec Ruins, near Farmington in northwestern New Mexico, preserves the ruins of one of the largest pre-Spanish villages in the Southwest, a 12th-century Indian town.

Badlands, in southwestern South Dakota, is an area of color-banded cliffs and pinnacles, and of prehistoric animal fossils.

Bandelier, in northern New Mexico near Santa Fe, is beautiful canyon country containing many cliff and open pueblo ruins of late prehistoric period.

Big Hole Battlefield, in southwestern Montana, was scene of tragic battle of the Indian Wars of the 1870's that were part of the winning of the West.

Black Canyon of the Gunnison, in southwestern Colorado near Montrose, is the spectacular gorge of the Gunnison River, notable for its narrowness, depth, ruggedness, and great expanses of sheer walls of granite, varying in color from black to pink.

Cabrillo, in southern California, on San Diego Bay, commemorates the discovery of the coast of California on Sept. 28, 1542, by Juan Rodriguez Cabrillo.

Canyon de Chelly, in northeast Arizona, retains in its red-walled cliffs evidence of a thousand years of prehistoric occupation by pueblo cliff-dweller Indians.

Capitol Reef, in southern Utah, is a region of sandstone cliffs, 20 miles long, brightly colored and carved by the elements into weird and fanciful figures.

Photo: Grand Canyon, by Chuck Abbott (Rapho-Guillumette)

Capulin Mountain, in northeastern New Mexico, is a large volcanic cinder cone which last erupted some 2,000 years ago.

Casa Grande, in southern Arizona, is an adobe tower, four stories high, built by Indian farmers of the Gila Valley 600 years ago.

Castillo de San Marcos, in St. Augustine, Florida, is an ancient fortification dating from the Spanish Colonial period.

Castle Clinton, in New York City, was harbor fort, famous "Castle Garden," an immigrant depot, fabulous aquarium, and is now being made into national monument.

Castle Pinckney was part of the early harbor defenses of Charleston, S.C.

Cedar Breaks, in southwestern Utah, near Cedar City, is a great natural amphitheater eroded into the 2,000-foot-thick Pink Cliffs of the Wasatch formation.

Chaco Canyon, in northwestern New Mexico, is one of the outstanding archaeological areas of the U.S., with more than a dozen large Indian ruins and hundreds of smaller sites.

Channel Islands, off southern California, is playland for sea lions and birds. The monument includes Santa Barbara and Anacapa Islands.

Chiricahua, in southeastern Arizona, has weirdly beautiful pinnacles and columns, eroded in volcanic rocks.

Colorado National Monument, in western part of the state near Grand Junction, has fantastically eroded and vividly colored highlands.

Craters of the Moon, in southern Idaho, has volcanic cones, craters, lava flows which make the land look like the moon as seen through a telescope.

Custer Battlefield, in southern Montana, was site of famous battle of the Little Bighorn River, "Custer's Last Stand."

Photo: Yosemite Valley, by Phillip Knight

403

Death Valley is situated in the rugged desert region of eastern California and southwestern Nevada. It is the lowest land area in the U.S., reaching 282 feet below sea level. Has distinctive desert vegetation and weird natural phenomena.

Devils Postpile, in central California, southeast of Yosemite, contains basaltic columns, some 60 feet high.

Devils Tower, in northeast Wyoming, is 865-foot tower of rock, evidence of volcanic activity millions of years ago.

Dinosaur National Monument, on the Utah-Colorado border, near Vernal, Utah, has the nation's richest fossil quarries.

Effigy Mounds, in northeastern Iowa, are outstanding examples of Indian mounds in shapes of animals and birds.

El Morro, in western New Mexico, is a sandstone monolith, also known as Inscription Rock, where Spanish explorers and early American emigrants carved messages.

Fort Frederica, off southeastern Georgia, was base for General Oglethorpe's military operations against the Spanish.

Fort Jefferson, off southern Florida, was largest of the 19th-century American coastal forts, and at one time "Key to the Gulf of Mexico."

Fort Laramie, in eastern Wyoming, was fur-trade post and guardian of covered wagon trails to Oregon, Utah, California.

Fort Matanzas, in northeastern Florida, was built by Spanish in 1737 to protect the back door to St. Augustine.

Fort McHenry, Maryland, was built to protect Baltimore's harbor. Its successful defense against British attack in 1814 inspired the "Star-Spangled Banner."

Fort Pulaski, in southeastern Georgia, was massive 19th-century fort on Cockspur Island. Attack by federal rifled cannon in 1862 showed ineffectiveness of old-style masonry fortifications.

Fort Sumter, at Charleston, South Carolina, was scene of the bombardment which began the Civil War, on April 12, 1861.

Fort Vancouver, in southwestern Washington, made a national monument in 1954, commemorates the fort's significant role as fur-trading headquarters and military outpost in the settlement and development of the Pacific northwest.

Fossil Cycad National Monument, in southwestern South Dakota, near Hot Springs, is an area in the Black Hills containing fossilized plants.

George Washington Birthplace, on the Potomac River in Virginia, 38 miles east of Fredericksburg, was plantation where George Washington was born and where he spent his first three years.

George Washington Carver National Monument, in southwestern Missouri, was birthplace of one who rose from slavery to become a world-famous scientist and benefactor of mankind.

Photo: Cedar Breaks National Monument, by Hubert A. Lowman

Gila Cliff Dwellings, in southwestern New Mexico, near Silver City, are well-preserved dwellings in 150-foot cliff.

Glacier Bay, in southeastern Alaska, contains great tidewater glaciers.

Gran Quivira, in central New Mexico, is impressive stone ruin of a frontier Spanish mission of the late 17th century.

Grand Canyon National Monument, in northwestern Arizona, adjoins Grand Canyon National Park on the west. It includes forty miles of the canyon.

Great Sand Dunes, in southern Colorado, is an area of shifting sand dunes entrapped by the great hook of the Sangre de Cristo Mountains.

Homestead, in southeastern Nebraska, is site of the first "claim" under the Homestead Act of 1862.

Hovenweep, in southeastern Utah on the Colorado line, contains four groups of remarkable prehistoric towers, pueblos, and cliff dwellings.

Jewel Cave National Monument, in the Black Hills of southwestern South Dakota, consists of limestone caves and chambers connected by narrow galleries.

Joshua Tree National Monument, near Indio in southeastern California, preserves typical desert country, with magnificent stands of Joshua-tree, cholla cactus, and other desert flora.

Katmai, in southern Alaska, includes the site of a recent volcanic eruption, the Valley of Ten Thousand Smokes and the stump of exploded Mount Katmai.

Lava Beds, in northern California, is an area of volcanic formations and the scene of the Modoc Indian War of 1872–73.

Photo: Half Dome, Yosemite Valley, by Ansel Adams

Lehman Caves, in eastern Nevada near Ely, is an intricate, vast cavern system underlying the flank of 13,061-foot Wheeler Peak in the high desert country.

Meriwether Lewis National Monument, in central Tennessee, is grave of the leader of the Lewis and Clark expedition that first carried the American flag across the continent to the Pacific, in 1804–5.

Montezuma Castle, in central Arizona, is one of our best preserved and most interesting cliff dwellings.

Mound City Group, in south central Ohio near Chillicothe, is a famous group of prehistoric Indian mounds.

Muir Woods, in western California just north of San Francisco, preserves a virgin stand of redwoods, the tallest of living things. Tallest specimen is 364 feet.

Natural Bridges, in southeastern Utah, contains three gigantic natural bridges. The highest has a span of 261 feet, and is 222 feet above the stream bed.

Navajo, in northeastern Arizona, is a national monument protecting three of the largest and most intricate of cliff dwellings, Betatakin, Keet Seel, and Inscription House.

Ocmulgee, in central Georgia near Macon, preserves a major Indian village that was occupied repeatedly through 10,000 years.

Old Kasaan, in southeastern Alaska, is site of abandoned Haida Indian village.

Oregon Caves, in southwestern Oregon, are limestone caverns of great beauty and variety.

Organ Pipe Cactus National Monument, in southern Arizona, west of Tucson, is a magnificent natural expanse of desert, with organ pipe cactus and other desert growth unique in the region.

Perry's Victory Memorial, in northern Ohio, is site of Commodore Perry's great victory in War of 1812, at Put-In Bay.

Petrified Forest, in eastern Arizona, has the greatest and most colorful concentration of petrified wood known in the world.

Pinnacles, in southern California, is an area of spirelike rock formations, 500 to 1,200 feet high, with caves and a variety of volcanic features.

Pipe Spring, in northwestern Arizona, near the Grand Canyon, is well-preserved Mormon fort. Monument commemorates a significant phase of the great westward movement by American pioneers.

Pipestone National Monument, in southwestern Minnesota, contains the quarries from which Plains Indians obtained the red stone preferred for peace pipes.

Rainbow Bridge, in southern Utah, is large enough to straddle the Capitol in Washington. A 278-foot span, it arches to a height of 309 feet—the largest known natural bridge in the world.

Saguaro National Monument, in southeastern Arizona, near Tucson, is a weird forest of fluted cacti.

Scotts Bluff, a landmark on the Oregon Trail, was a favorite campsite and a great natural highway to the Far West. It is in western Nebraska.

Sitka, in southeastern Alaska, is site of Indian defeat by the Russian settlers.

Statue of Liberty, on Bedloe's Island in New York harbor, was a gift from the people of France to the people of the United States. It commemorates the U.S.-French alliance during the American Revolution and symbolizes freedom and democracy.

Sunset Crater, in northern Arizona, near Flagstaff, is volcanic cone so highly colored as to give appearance of sunset.

Timpanogos Cave, in north central Utah, near Salt Lake City, is series of small but beautifully decorated underground chambers within limestone beds.

Tonto National Monument, in south central Arizona, protects 14th-century cliff dwellings of tribe who were among finest craftsmen of prehistoric Pueblo Indians.

Tumacacori National Monument preserves historic Spanish Catholic mission. It is in southern Arizona, north of Nogales.

Tuzigoot National Monument, in central Arizona, contains remnants of prehistoric fortified town of Indians who farmed the Verde Valley for two centuries, from 1100 to 1300 A.D.

Photo: Betatakin Ruin, Navajo National Monument, by Bert Vaughn (Shostal)   **407**

Photo: Mount Mitchell Intersection on Blue Ridge Parkway, western North Carolina

Verendrye National Monument, in northwestern North Dakota, commemorates the explorations of Pierre Verendrye and his three sons.

Walnut Canyon, in northern Arizona, near Flagstaff, is site of hundreds of little 13th-century cliff dwellings, constructed by their Indian builders in the hollow caves of a steep canyon.

White Sands, in south central New Mexico, near Alamogordo, is one of the world's strangest deserts, with huge gypsum dunes of purest white. Driven by the active southwest winds, the sand dunes are constantly changing.

Whitman National Monument, in southeastern Washington, near Walla Walla, is site where Marcus and Narissa Whitman ministered to the spiritual and physical needs of the Cayuse Indians and the immigrants of the Oregon Trail.

Wupatki National Monument, in northern Arizona, north of Flagstaff, contains many 11th-century pueblos of red sandstone, gleaming against black basaltic cliffs.

Yucca House, in southwestern Colorado, near Cortez, preserves prehistoric Indian village whose inhabitants had high skill in pottery and weaving.

Zion National Monument, in southwestern Utah, adjoins Zion National Park on the northwest. It includes eight canyons, of which Kolob is the largest and almost as spectacular as Zion Canyon itself. It also includes famous Hurricane Fault.

NATIONAL MILITARY PARKS

Chickamauga and Chattanooga, in northwestern Georgia and eastern Tennessee, includes the battlefields of Chickamauga, Orchard Knob, Lookout Mountain and Missionary Ridge, important in the Civil War's Chattanooga campaign of 1863.

Fort Donelson, in northern Tennessee, was important in the western campaigns of the Civil War. Its fall in 1862 gave Grant the title of "Unconditional Surrender."

Fredericksburg and Spotsylvania, in northern Virginia, memorializes four major engagements of the Civil War, the Battles of Chancellorsville, Fredericksburg, the Wilderness, and Spotsylvania Court House. No other area of comparable size on the American continent has seen such heavy and continuous fighting.

Gettysburg, in southern Pennsylvania, was scene of the decisive Battle of Gettysburg, on July 1, 2 and 3, 1863, marking the turning point of the Civil War, and the place where Abraham Lincoln made his celebrated Gettysburg Address.

Guilford Courthouse is in central North Carolina, near Greensboro. Here, on March 15, 1781, Cornwallis won a victory over Greene's American forces, but was so weakened as a result that the British soon afterward took the road to Yorktown and final surrender.

Kings Mountain, in northern South Carolina, marked the climax of a victorious rising of American frontiersmen against British and Tories in the Carolina foothills in 1780 which foreshadowed the British military defeats of 1781.

Moores Creek, in southeastern North Carolina, near Wilmington, is known as "the Lexington and Concord of the South." The Battle of Moores Creek Bridge, in 1776, was a complete victory for the Patriots over the Loyalist element in the state.

Petersburg, in southeastern Virginia, was the scene of the decisive military operations that cut Confederate lines of communication between Richmond and the South and led to the capture of the Confederate capital.

Shiloh, in southern Tennessee, was scene of the first major engagement in the western campaigns of the Civil War. It opened the way for the Union forces to gain possession of the Mississippi River during the following year and to split the Confederacy with the capture of Vicksburg.

Stones River, in central Tennessee, was the first big battle in the Northern

strategy of cutting the Confederacy in two by driving eastward to the sea. Three-day battle began Dec. 31, 1862.

Vicksburg, in western Mississippi, commemorates the 47-day siege of Vicksburg in 1863 which gave the North control of the Mississippi, splitting the Confederacy asunder.

Photo: Jefferson Memorial, Washington, D.C., by Fred H. Ragsdale

NATIONAL MEMORIAL PARK

Theodore Roosevelt National Memorial Park recognizes Theodore Roosevelt's service to his nation in conserving its natural resources. It is located in southwestern North Dakota.

NATIONAL BATTLEFIELD PARKS

Kennesaw Mountain, in northwestern part of Georgia, near Marietta, was the scene of two heavy assaults by General W. T. Sherman in his Atlanta campaign. In the first battle Sherman failed to break the Confederate lines and suffered heavy losses. He then resumed the flanking movements which had won his previous successes, and forced the Confederates to retire to the vicinity of Atlanta.

Manassas (Bull Run) National Battlefield Park is in northern Virginia. Here was fought the opening field battle of the Civil War, First Manassas, often called "Bull Run" after the small stream in the vicinity. Second Manassas, a year later, was a Confederate victory and led to Lee's first invasion of the North.

Richmond National Battlefield Park, Virginia, was the scene of several battles in defense of the Capital of the Confederacy during the Civil War. The park includes portions of the battlefields of Cold Harbor and Malvern Hill.

NATIONAL BATTLEFIELD SITES

Antietam, in western Maryland, was scene of the battle which brought to an end General Robert E. Lee's first invasion of the North in 1862.

Brices Cross Roads, in northeastern Mississippi, north of Tupelo, commemorates 1864 battle in which Confederates under General Forrest brilliantly routed a Union force.

Cowpens, in northwestern South Carolina, marks the battle in which the British under Tarleton were defeated by Daniel Morgan, in 1781.

Fort Necessity, in southwestern Pennsylvania, commemorates Washington's first major battle and the opening engagement of the 7-year struggle between England and France for the control of America.

Tupelo, in northeastern Mississippi, marks attempt of Confederates to advance on General Sherman's line of communications.

White Plains, in southeastern New York, commemorates American Revolution battle on Chatterton Hill.

NATIONAL HISTORIC SITES

Adams Mansion, at Quincy, Massachusetts, was the home of Presidents John Adams and John Quincy Adams; Charles Francis Adams, U.S. minister to Great Britain during the Civil War, and his four sons, one of whom wrote the American classic, *The Education of Henry Adams.*

Federal Hall Memorial, at Wall and Nassau streets in New York City, was first Capitol of the U.S.A.

Fort Raleigh, on Roanoke Island off North Carolina, was the scene of Sir Walter Raleigh's ill-fated attempts to establish an English colony in America, and birthplace of the first English child born in the New World.

Hampton, at Towson, a suburb of Baltimore, Maryland, is one of the great Georgian houses of America, built 1783–90, and restored in 1948.

Home of Franklin D. Roosevelt, at Hyde Park, New York, was birthplace, home and "summer White House" of President Franklin D. Roosevelt. Nearby are his Rose Garden grave, and the Museum and Library.

Hopewell Village, in southeastern Pennsylvania, represents the early manorial iron-making communities from which came the great iron and steel industry of America today.

Jefferson National Expansion Memorial, at St. Louis, Missouri, marks the westward growth of America and preserves one of the principal gateways to the West.

Old Philadelphia Custom House, in downtown Philadelphia, Pennsylvania, is a fine example of Greek revival architecture, and noted as the second bank of the United States.

Salem Maritime, bordering on Salem Harbor, Massachusetts, memorializes American maritime greatness, the outgrowth of pioneering enterprise on the sea.

San Juan, Puerto Rico, consists of massive masonry fortifications begun by the Spanish in the 16th century, the oldest European-type defenses in U.S. territory.

Vanderbilt Mansion, Hyde Park, New York, overlooking the Hudson River, is a fine example of the palatial U.S. residence of the 1880–1900 period.

NATIONAL MEMORIALS

Coronado, on southern border of Arizona, shows the route by which Coronado came on his famous explorations in 1540.

De Soto, at Shaw's Point, four miles west of Bradenton on the west coast of Florida, marks probable landing place of Hernando de Soto in 1539.

Fort Caroline, in northeastern Florida, near Jacksonville, marks the site of early French settlement and beginning of struggle between French and Spanish.

House Where Lincoln Died, Washington, D.C., has been refurnished to give the atmosphere of a typical home of the 1860's. Lincoln was brought here from Ford's Theater, and died on April 15, 1865.

Lee Mansion, in Arlington National Cemetery, Virginia, became the home of Robert E. Lee when he married Mary Custis. Here he wrote his resignation from the U. S. Army to join the cause of the South.

Photo: Lincoln Museum, Washington, D.C., formerly Ford's Theater, by Ankers

Photo: Lincoln Memorial, Washington, D.C., by Capt. M. W. Arps, U.S.N. Ret. **413**

Lincoln Memorial, Washington, D.C., is a classical structure of great beauty, with 20-foot seated figure of Abraham Lincoln, the Great Emancipator.

Lincoln Museum, Washington, D.C., was formerly Ford's Theater, in which the President was shot by John Wilkes Booth. The museum now contains many books, letters, documents, photos and objects that pertain to Lincoln's life.

Mount Rushmore, in the Black Hills of South Dakota, bears on its 6,000-foot-high granite face the likenesses of four great Americans, George Washington, Thomas Jefferson, Abraham Lincoln and Theodore Roosevelt. Gutzon Borglum did the models and directed the work of carving the 60-foot heads.

Thomas Jefferson Memorial, Washington, D.C., is circular colonnaded rotunda in the classic style introduced to the U.S. by Jefferson. Interior walls contain inscriptions based on his writings.

Washington Monument, in Washington, D.C., is a 555-foot obelisk which dominates the U.S. capital. Built between 1848 and 1885, it shows the gratitude of the people of the U.S. to the father of their country, George Washington.

Wright Brothers National Memorial was known, until 1953, as Kill Devil Hill Monument. It is located on a barrier beach off northern North Carolina, near Kitty Hawk. Here was made the first successful power-driven airplane flight in history, on Dec. 17, 1903.

NATIONAL PARKWAYS

Blue Ridge Parkway leads from the end of Skyline Drive, in Shenandoah Na-

Photo: Lee Mansion, Arlington Cemetery, Virginia, by Capt. M. W. Arps, U.S.N. Ret.

tional Park, Virginia, to Asheville, North Carolina and the Great Smoky Mountains National Park. It is not an express parkway, but a scenic high road which averages 3,000 feet above sea level and is designed for the leisurely tourist.

George Washington Memorial Parkway runs along the Potomac from Washington to Mount Vernon. When finished, it will embrace many interesting landmarks, in Virginia and Maryland, connected with the life of George Washington.

Photo: Washington Monument, and Cherry Trees in Blossom around Tidal Basin

Natchez Trace Parkway, in Tennessee, Alabama and Mississippi, follows the Indian trails that became a wilderness roadway between Natchez and Nashville, and later a post road and highway. When completed, the parkway will be 450 miles in length.

Suitland Parkway connects Washington, D.C., with Andrews air base, Maryland.

NATIONAL CAPITAL PARKS

National Capital Parks include more than 770 parks in the District of Columbia and nearby Virginia and Maryland. They total more than 29,000 acres.

Photo: Air view of Washington, D.C.